THIRTEENTH
YEAR IN ZION

.

THIRTEENTH YEAR IN ZION

MORMONS CONFRONT THE TWENTY-FIRST CENTURY

DUANE KEOWN

Library of Congress Control Number:		2012917603
ISBN:	Hardcover	978-1-4797-2107-8
	Softcover	978-1-4797-2106-1
	Ebook	978-1-4797-2108-5

To order additional copies of this book, contact:
Xlibris Corporation
1-888-795-4274
www.Xlibris.com
Orders@Xlibris.com

CONTENTS

ACKNOWLEDGMENTS

First, I recognize my lifelong friend Wayne Hansen, retired special education teacher and builder of everything, who ventured with me into Zion in June of 1957 for an impulsive and cursory look at Brigham Young University. Just over a year later, in 1958, we began the fall academic quarter at BYU. It was our shared life-changing adventure. Through the years, usually around a fishing trip, we reminisce about events during our school years at the Y. Mormon behaviors, many with only faith for their cause, usually trigger our conversations about the Saints. Today they still bring puzzlement, but more smiles with our age and distance from Utah.

My first wife, Betty Pearson, through the San Juan County, Utah, years and mother of my two children, endured with me the hills and valleys of the interface with the Mormons. We look back with pride how well the family survived the marriage ending. The time, our families, and the culture that surrounded our marriage funneled us down a path unhappy to follow. These pressures and influences subsided after leaving Utah and our home range.

Thanks to Jeff for many suggestions and thoroughly reading the manuscript. Jeff Lockwood is an award-winning entomologist turned philosopher and creative writing professor at the University of Wyoming, whom I have known since his arrival at UW in 1986. His essays have been honored with a Pushcart Prize, a John Burroughs Award, the Albert Schweitzer Sermon Award of the Unitarian Universalist Association, and inclusion in Best American Science and Nature Writing.

Barbara Chatton is a friend, colleague, and legendary retired professor of children's literature at the University of Wyoming. Her retirement brought a large crowd to acknowledge twenty-eight years of service to the university and the College of Education. Her literary gifts of a wide variety went to children and adults in Wyoming and beyond. Most recently, for me and my manuscript, her gift was to improve the clarity of the story I tell.

I do not know whom or what to thank for my seeing the world differently than Mormons who surrounded me while immersed in the LDS culture. My mother and an older sister, who are both deceased, and my younger sister, who lives in California, are Southern Baptists. My father, also deceased, would go to church regularly with them but was never a joiner. Professors especially influenced me by looking for the causes for humankind's successes and dilemmas. They were not so willing to thank God or blame the devil. But it was Mormonism that opened my religion-skeptical eyes.

Twenty years after the first marriage, I married again. Finally, appreciation goes to my wife, Joy, naturalist, science teacher, and watercolor artist, who is always the first reader of what I write. She keeps me in balance with the credit I give to science and her Christian religion. Her energy, enthusiasm, and love of the natural world were my rare find.

INTRODUCTION

We were on our way to a "Successful Schools" workshop in Park City, Utah. It was 1975. I was the only non-Mormon school administrator in the car with the Latter-day Saint public school leaders from San Juan School District, in the southeastern corner of Utah. It was near Moab, Utah, when Galen Donan, the high school principal from Monticello, started the conversation about an educator in Moab whom the passengers in the car were acquainted. I didn't know the man and wouldn't have remembered his name. But the ensuing conversation is vividly remembered years after the ride to Park City. Donan said, "How would you feel if your daughter told you she was going to marry a Negro?" Such was the case of the Mormon parent in Moab. Donan knew the sentiments of the Mormons aboard before he asked the question. In 1975, blacks could not hold the sacred Mormon priesthood, and that denied them nearly all of the privileges of white males in the church: going on missions, baptizing members, ever having true authority in the church. A fifteen-year-old white deacon had more authority than a black man. And even today, women do not hold the priesthood.

That morning, John Bynum, the recently appointed director of the new technical school in Blanding, put the parent's dilemma and membership in the church into perspective. He said, "I could handle it if he was a member of the church. I wouldn't care if he was a Lamanite." Lamanite is the Mormon term for American Indian. According to Latter-day Saint theology, blacks and American Indians are the recipients of curses by God on their progenitors.

For me, the conversation of the school administrators wasn't unexpected. After thirteen years in Utah and a Brigham Young University education, I knew the value and life meaning Mormons took from their church, even with its racial biases and theological absurdities. How did these beliefs and debasing behaviors their scriptures propagate come to be, and why must they remain? When LDS missionaries knock on doors around the world to recruit new members to the faith, theirs is the insider's story. Mine is the outsider's story.

In 1830, when the Church of Jesus Christ of Latter-day Saints had its official beginning, science was called natural philosophy. Charles Darwin and Alfred Wallace had not yet discovered the principles of natural selection that power the adaptation and change of species. Chemistry was in its infancy. Geology, the age of the earth, and the meaning of the layers of sediment that compose much of the earth's crust and tell its history had not yet taken full meaning. Gregor Mendel was more than twenty years from beginning experiments with pea plants. It was the Age of Enlightenment, the era in Western philosophical, intellectual, scientific, and cultural life in which reason was advocated as the primary source for legitimacy of knowledge and authority. Yet in Upstate New York, Joseph Smith, an uneducated farm boy and founder of the Church of Jesus Christ of Latter-day Saints, was giving answers to scientific questions and cultural history without the benefit of scientific methodology or a science education, such as it was in the early nineteenth century. He claimed that answers were given to him by an angel, answers to questions such as why American Indians have darker skins than northern Europeans and specifics about the pre-Columbian peopling of the Americas. He said that through himself, the angel, whom he called Moroni, directed the recovery of an ancient history of the first Americans. According to the *Documentary History of the Church,* Smith said the record was on golden plates that were taken from a hill called Cumorah, near his home, a local landmark close to Palmyra, New York. The record told about a tribe from Israel that crossed the sea in submarine-like boats and populated the Western world about 600 BC, following the Fall of Babylon in Old Testament times. They came with European livestock, farm implements made of iron, and they spoke languages of the Middle East. Smith said he transcribed the history of the tribe and its descendants from the golden plates by peering into two magical stones, the Urim and Thummim. He later said that the writing on the plates was in "reformed Egyptian" and the plates were returned to the angel. His transcription of the record became *The Book of Mormon,* which he later said "is the most correct of any book on earth, and the keystone of our religion, and a man would get nearer to God by abiding by its precepts than by any other book."[1] (*Documentary History of the Church,* volume IV, p. 461) He was able to convince some of his family and friends of the authenticity of his experience and thus began the Latter-day Saints (Mormon) Church. Today, the church has more than fourteen million members.

Throughout *The Book of Mormon,* God curses the Lamanites, the forerunners of today's Americans Indians, with dark skin because of their sins. In later revelations, Smith gave his followers the reasons blacks are "cursed" with dark skin. According to the Mormon prophet's revelations, like the Lamanites, modern blacks must bear the black skin as the mark of their ancestors' iniquities. Followers believe this history is an authoritative scripture from God, revealed through their organizer and first prophet. A revelation was needed in 1978 following civil rights protests almost daily by blacks and others concerning the LDS Church not allowing people of African origin to hold their sacred priesthood. Human rights marches around the Salt Lake Temple and the national attention of major universities refusing to schedule Brigham Young University for athletic events threatened the very existence of the church. Spencer Kimball, through his claimed communication with God, revealed that blacks could now hold the sacred priesthood. The revelation was more than convenient. It was arguably for the church's survival. America had passed such an abomination both in law and anthropological understanding. Kimball's revelation highlighted the age-old religious problem of claiming absolute knowledge.

With the exception of the most fundamental believers, modern Christians as well as the faithful of other world religions use some discretion as they look to their holy scriptures for truths about our existence. They realize their guiding words were written when civilization was very young and that many stories and parables may be symbolic of human relationships. That the Bible does not have literal inerrancy does not trouble most Christians. But relative to the Bible, the Mormon scriptures are hot off the press. Most of the original revelations are in the possession of the church and are in Joseph Smith's own handwriting.

Religions that proclaim absolute truths are forever in conflict with the findings of science. There are vast ranges of certainty within which falls the accumulated knowledge of science. From the working models at the frontiers of our understanding to the observable facts that become the framework, all of our information fits somewhere in this spectrum of certainty. In his article, "Age of the Earth and the Universe," George O. Abell explains,

> There is always a frontier beyond which we have yet no understanding and at which our understanding is incomplete. At and near the frontier, our models are subject to modification, perhaps rejection, as new information becomes available. But the distance of uncertainty at the frontier does not negate our knowledge in the well-trodden foreground. Whether or not neutrinos turn out to have finite rest mass, for example has no bearing on the motion of the earth about the sun.[2] ("The Age of the Earth and Universe," George O. Abell, from *Scientists Confront Creationists,* pp. 34–35, W. W. Norton & Company, 1983)

In the twenty-first century, much of the science from which Mormons must defend their beliefs is in the "well-trodden foreground." The human species is very old relative to the events of Genesis: Adam and Eve, Noah's Flood, and *The Book of Mormon* in its entirety. Diversity in species or races of humans is well understood biologically and does not occur because of curses by God. The same principles that explain diversity in other species apply to us. The blacks and American Indians' skin color does not fit Smith's explanation, and no biologist, not even the most devout Mormon biologist, would submit Smith's authoritative explanation for scientific review. And we wait for a revelation to free American Indians from the church's dismal explanation for their biological differences.

Organic evolution in the twenty-first century is among the very well-understood naturally occurring processes. Joseph Smith gave his followers

God's explanation for the peopling of the Americas. Today, matching of DNA types has become the most reliable evidence in following the origin paths of earth's human populations. Though believable at the time by biblical literalists, Smith's answers no longer make sense to the modern sciences of genetics, archeology, and anthropology. The evidence given by these disciplines takes the first Americans back to Eastern Asia, and their migrations are also in the well-trodden foreground realm of science.

Because Joseph Smith claimed to speak for God through revelations, Mormons are locked in time and faith, without further revelations to modify, correct, or add to their holy scriptures. Joseph Smith was an uneducated farm boy on the frontier of the United States and out of touch with the intellectual revolution that was astir in his time. It was indeed an anachronism that Mormonism in the early nineteenth century was linking its theology with the scriptures of the Old Testament at the very time when the stage was being set for an explosion of information about our human relationship with life and the planet.

In the summer of 1957, with my friend Wayne Hansen, I wandered into Utah quite by chance in search of a college to attend. Wayne and I were leaving Western State College in Gunnison, Colorado, for a university that offered more biology. The border of Utah might have been Montana, South Dakota, or any other Western state. The knowledge I had of Utah, Mormons, and Brigham Young University was very minimal. Being a sports enthusiast, I knew BYU had a reputation for producing good basketball teams, although in those years their football team was hardly competitive. Our high school U.S. history book had the requisite paragraphs about Mormon persecution in the Midwest, the settlement of Utah—Brigham Young reaching the Great Basin of

Utah and declaring, "This is the place." I was aware of the conflicts the LDS had with American society in practicing polygamy and that they gave up the practice to join the Union. I was relatively unbiased and interested to learn more about Mormonism when I entered BYU a year later. Students attending the Y, as it is known throughout Mormon society, are required to attend a religion course each semester, and these courses are mostly about Mormon theology and history. The beginning of thirteen years I spent in Utah was the fall of 1958. There were three years at BYU, where I graduated with a Bachelor of Science degree in zoology in 1962. The three BYU years were interrupted when I was out of money and went into the southern Utah canyon country to teach all the elementary grades in a one-room school at the Hideout Mine. It was uranium boom time in southern Utah, and there were many isolated schools near the mines and few teachers willing to venture into the desolation of the mine sites. At the Hideout, I learned about "Jack Mormons," Mormons in heart and head who do not practice the rigid principles of the faith, as well as the gentile (non-Mormon) miners of Utah. After finishing at BYU, there was a year teaching at Aneth, Utah in the Utah region of the Navajo Indian Reservation. I was broke again after completing undergraduate studies and San Juan County, rich in mineral resources, had the best pay in Utah. At Aneth, I had a ringside seat to learn about Mormonism and its relationship with American Indians. Indians to Mormons are Lamanites, a fallen and cursed lot according to *The Book of Mormon*. After a master's in biology at Colorado State University, I returned to the Mormon town of Monticello, Utah as the biology and other sciences teacher in the high school. After five years, I began a doctoral program at Ball State University in Muncie, Indiana. It was the golden years for science education and successful science teachers were given generous scholarships to return for graduate classes to advance school science.

We were behind the Russians, and the National Science Foundation's goal was for the United States to catch and pass the USSR. It was Cold War times. I earned the doctorate, again in biology, with a minor in natural resources. I also earned an endorsement to be a secondary school administrator. With the doctorate completed in two years, our family couldn't wait to return to the beloved Four Corners Country with what I thought was full understanding of how to live in the Mormon-dominated society. Back in Utah, I became the principal of the San Juan County Junior High School in Blanding, twenty-five miles south of Monticello. In Blanding, I learned that I did not have the skills or the tolerance to accept without skirmishes the Mormon-dominated society. In those small communities, I developed a love-hate relationship with Mormonism—love for the children so respectful of teachers and their parents, and hate was for the stereotyped Mormon vision of the world students of public school age already had. They were only beginning to learn about the earth, its people, and themselves. That has been the catalyst that fires my desire to tell the story. Is there an escape for the innocent children to see their culture and religion from the vantage I was afforded?

Now retired, after thirty years a science education professor at the University of Wyoming, I am back into the world of Mormons, but only briefly to write this book. The manuscript was begun soon after I left Utah. The memories of the events that begin each chapter were vivid then and recorded. At the university, I waited for the first sabbatical leave and headed for Utah to write about Utah experiences. Professional duties at the University of Wyoming and zeal to save our environment consumed me for decades, and environmental issues still do.

In retrospect the thirty-year delay in writing about the LDS is fortunate.

I began the journey as naively as some Mormons I met along the way. For me, I grew into questioning and awareness based upon my education, experiences, and encounters with a wide variety of people I met. Then, "Why wade back into that swamp?" a friend asked me. "I have always been a teacher," I said. My Utah history and Utah experiences, in combination with a science education, allows me to give an outsider perspective of LDS theology and cultural behavior in relationship with modern science and American idealism. And the book goes to fundamentalist religions with their faithful followings who are locked on absolutes that cause strife and will not allow them to realize what it means to be fully human. Understanding of our species is dynamic.

For the reader, I will interchangeably refer to Mormons as the LDS, Latter-day Saints, or the Saints. When you hear Utah, it could be Deseret, which was the first name for the Mormon-settled territory, or Zion, a name dear to the pioneer Saints. Mormondom will refer to the Mormons and their faith world over. Throughout the book, American Indians is chosen for use rather than Native Americans. Blacks is used instead of Afro Americans, which restricts the location of these people. The real names of many of the people have been changed.

CHAPTER 1

ALIEN IN DESERET

Brigham Young University

Ninety-seven percent of you are LDS. Of the other three percent who are not LDS, most will be LDS when they graduate.

—Ernest Wilkinson, president of BYU, before a
student assembly in the fall of 1958

It was in January 1959 and the first preseason baseball practice at Brigham Young University was ending, as we players did the required laps around the track in the Joseph Smith Field House. I was really tired. It must have been workouts like this one that earned the team a berth in the NCAA baseball playoffs last year. The cleats of the baseball shoes scraped the pavement on the route across the parking lot to the lockers and showers. I knew why the last season ended for the Cougars, and it wasn't because they weren't good enough. It was because a game in the NCAA tournament progression was scheduled on Sunday. The authorities of the LDS Church would not allow the Y team to play. The team concurred with little dissension. It was national news. The Y academic team in the TV program *College Bowl* that was on Sunday afternoons the same year was allowed to participate. "Why was this?" I asked. I acknowledge my bias, but baseball is a finesse game of running, throwing, catching, hitting the ball, and knowing what to do with the ball. College bowl was a game of recall of facts, not reasoning.

The clicking of the cleats on the pavement of the many prospects for the team sounded like a beginning tap dance class. Bob Thompson, a high school shortstop from Washington state, walked with me. In short sentences caused by the many laps around the field house track, we talked with excitement about our impressions of this first practice. Bob and I were both walk-ons and humbled by the talent around us. Bob and I became basement mates at 840 North Fifth Street back in September.

As the players entered the locker room, the clatter of cleats on the concrete became louder. The walls lined with lockers contained the sound. There wasn't much different about this locker room than the one at Western State College where I had been a sophomore in 1957. Lockers slammed shut with the same familiar clank, and in the background, there were echo chamber sounds from the shower room. At least half of the aspiring players were wearing what appeared to be the same style of underwear. It was one piece, cut at the bottom between the knee and the thigh, short sleeved, and with small patches on the chest—right over the nipples. Hell! Maybe this was part of the regular BYU baseball uniform, and only the lettermen wore them. I didn't know it, but this was my first look at the underwear the LDS call garments. Some with the underwear looked a bit older. I was uncertain. It wasn't the first time since September that a Mormon manner or custom separated me from the student body, which was 97 percent Mormon. I showered and put on my Penny's Towncraft shorts. Bob and I walked across campus toward our sleeping rooms in the home basement.

I sat on the edge of my bed and picked some chords on the guitar that was an integral part of my portable belongings in those years. But damn! Those suits of underwear continued to bother me—it was physical, not a mannerism, and it concerned me as much as any of the many differences about these people.

I shared a basement room with Wayne Hansen who had been my sidekick since high school. I told Wayne about the strange underwear at baseball practice. I remember well his reaction: "God, don't you know about garments?" But Wayne didn't know about their religious significance, so we both headed down the hall to Bob's room. He was our Mormon buddy, interpreter, and confidante. He began his explanation with his usual prelude, "You probably won't understand this but…" And he was right. We didn't understand, because Bob knew little about garments. He went with the flow. He told us that garments are given to worthy Mormon men and women to wear for life when they receive their "endowments." This could only happen at sacred temples. The garments, he said, reminded the men and women to behave and always remember they are Mormons. Bob didn't wear garments. He had never been a missionary or gone to a temple. They are usually obtained at temples prior to, but not always, before the mission, or with marriage in the temple.

At the usual time that evening, Wayne hollered down the hall that his car, a '56 Pontiac, was headed up the hill to the campus for dinner. The best food that we had found was served at the cafeteria in the Joseph Smith Building. This was a large and beautiful multipurpose building near the south side of the campus. Meals always began for the patrons of BYU cafeterias with grace. For Wayne and me, we always felt conspicuous as our meals began. It would have been sociable for us to follow that old adage, "When in Rome…" But neither he nor I had ever been so amiable to follow without good cause. Social pressure weighed heavily upon the members to comply with the best LDS behavior at their churches' most idealized educational institution. Had Wayne and I conformed, it would have been hypocritical and only to escape the scorn. It wasn't imagined. If we quickly looked around the second before the first bite, we might meet the eyes of those who questioned our lack of reverence, especially the middle-aged ladies that handled the serving line. They came to know us and watched us to see if we might have joined the fold and were saying the prayers.

Wayne had lived a brief time in Provo when he was elementary age. His dad was a mechanic. He knew Mormon outward manners better than I. Mormons are known to the outside world for particular behaviors. They don't smoke or drink alcohol, coffee or tea. They build big churches and temples and the men, and now women too, go on missions in the church's attempt to convert the world to their faith. For a very disciplined two years, in pairs (a companionship), they tell their gospel story to all who will listen. Then they come home and raise large families. But Wayne was probably at my level in knowing Mormon theology.

That night after the first baseball practice, sleep would not come easily. It must have been cumulative: the prayers with so many occasions, the closed campus on Sundays, the expected Sunday missionaries, religion woven into so much of living, and now the garments. It seemed like every confounding experience that I had encountered with that American subculture was reconstructed in my mind. It was only a few days before, at the regular weekly religious assembly of the student body held on Wednesdays, the president of BYU, Ernest Wilkenson, talked about the conversion rate of non-LDS students to Mormonism. He said only 3 percent of the student body was non-Mormon, and that if they stayed to graduate, most of the 3 percent would be Mormon.

"Damn," I thought. If I stay at this place, my chances of remaining a gentile are mighty slim. But, what the hell. Something powerful must have drawn us to this place. What would be wrong with being Mormon? It would surely be more comfortable around here socially. My hang-up at that stage was the Joseph Smith story. I just couldn't accept the idea of golden plates being delivered by an angel from within a mountain to God's appointed earthly prophet, Joseph Smith. "Read *The Book of Mormon* with real intent and a sincere heart," the missionaries who visited us early and often had assured Wayne and me, "and the truth of these things will be made known to you." They were quoting from their gospel. And they would read that scripture to us—often.

What was it about this town and this campus that drew me here? It had been fifteen months since Wayne and I had spent the sixteen hours in Provo and seriously considered BYU. But I didn't have enough money to continue college in the fall of 1957. So after that visit, I traveled to Alaska and worked in an oilfield for a year, and Wayne returned to Western State. But since arriving to begin school at the Y, I had gone to sleep so many times with that thought tumbling in my mind. "Why was I here?" It was usually when some difference, my ignorance about Mormon ways, left me on the sideline feeling as an alien in Utah, the Mormon state. Once again, it went back to that summer in 1957 when Wayne and I decided to give that university a look.

My best friend Wayne and I had begun college at Western State College in Gunnison, Colorado. To attend Western State was a practical decision for me. I played a trumpet solo at a Fine Arts Festival in Durango, Colorado, the spring of my senior year in high school, and the Western State band director was the judge. I was given a scholarship. In the second year at Western State, my parents would have three children in college on a bookkeeper's wage. An additional reason to go there was that Tom Belt, my partner in leading the dance band we put together in high school, had chosen Western State. My parents were hardly in on the decision. I knew how financially stressed they would be. They had little advice to offer me and my sisters about college. Neither of my parents had much college experience. My mother had one year of college at Fort Lewis Junior College, and though my dad had a white-collar job, he had only a tenth grade education.

At Western State, Wayne Hansen's experience and mine were nearly parallel. He first planned to be dentist. I had no major but learned to love biology. The first year it seemed with each required class there was a new interest. First it was history with the influence of Dr. Syzmanski. Music was important. With Tom Belt, we reformed our dance band with new members and became the regular band at the Student Union on Wednesday nights. Then came the biology class with Dr. Walker. In retrospect, for both Wayne and me, biology had real answers to so many questions, and Dr. Walker gave us such confidence that answers to life's most important questions were just around the corner, in biology. In the summer of 1957, Wayne and I went looking for a larger college or university, with studying more biology in mind.

Summer vacation, 1957, had begun. It was a June day at the Point Lookout Conoco station where I was working. The gas pump bell rang, and I left my grease job in the bay. Point Lookout is the entrance to Mesa Verde National Park, and I hurried to pump gas and probably answer questions about the Four Corners Country or the Park. Nope, it was not a tourist this time. It was Kenny Baxtrom, a friend who had driven the ten miles from Cortez to tell me he was quitting his oil exploration job with Western Geophysical Company. If I hurried to the seismograph company's office, I could probably get the job he was leaving. I did just that and got the job. I wouldn't begin for a week. Wayne was working at his dad's auto repair shop. That evening, we mapped out our search for a new college. We would take the Gunnison Route and spend Saturday night in Gunnison, and Sunday, it would be off to Denver to look at schools along Colorado's eastern front. We knew Gunnison nightspots too well and got a late start Sunday morning for Denver.

Monday morning, we began in Boulder at Colorado University. CU, with native sandstone buildings overgrown with ivy, had the Ivy League look. Maybe too Ivy League for small-town guys. It wasn't the first choice for Cortez kids—too expensive and Cortez was mostly poor folk. Then came Colorado State College in Greeley—now called University of Northern Colorado. Only forty miles northwest was Colorado State University in Fort Collins. It was only late afternoon, and we had given the three Colorado universities a very cursory look. We were already backtracking toward Cortez. It was somewhere near Loveland that I said to Wayne that we had two or three days left. Why not head for Utah? That was it. In every life, so it is said, there is a crossroads, a decision that changes everything. The decision late that June day in 1957 was just such a turning point in our lives.

It was on to Denver and west on I-70. Just past Georgetown, we took U.S. 40 and would follow it to Heber City, Utah. Those were good days. We were so free. Thirty-cent gasoline, sleeping in campgrounds, and shaving in service stations. We were choosing a college and slowing down if girls along the way would smile. Decades later I realize what a superficial survey we made of the schools. I'm not sure we even picked up their catalogs.

Soon, we were coming down Rabbit Ears Pass into Steamboat Springs, Colorado. The glass-pack mufflers echoed off of the walls of road cuts, and in the valley below, there were forty shades of green splashed with little blue lakes where the snow from the white-capped peaks had drained for the summer. In June, the fields of that valley always appear to have been sprinkled with a fresh, soft cover of yellow dandelions. In Steamboat Springs, we bought a six-pack of beer. West of Craig, sagebrush began to dominate the rolling hills, and soon, there was the Utah boarder. It might as well have been the Montana border or the New Mexico border in that stage of our Mormon experience. There were forty-eight states then, and Utah was one of them. From Cortez, my family sometimes crossed the Utah border fifty miles to the west to visit my mother's brother, who married a Mormon girl. They lived in Monticello. She was a sweet, generous, and beautiful lady, and our family loved her. Uncle Fay and Aunt Barbara had five children. It was probably twenty years after the marriage before my uncle joined the Mormon Church. I never have belonged to a church. I knew Uncle Fay's family was Mormon and not Baptists, like my mother and sisters. Church, or school for that matter, was not high on my list of interests then. I thought baseball fields were built first, and schools with them were afterthoughts.

Wayne's Pontiac rolled west on U.S. 40 over the sagebrush-covered hills of northern Utah. Our destination for the night was Provo, and the little town of Vernal was just a short way beyond a few more hills. The air in that quiet little town at the foot of the Uinta Mountains was cool, and the sun was low behind the horizon. The look of an oil town had not captured the community or the economy yet. Oil would come in the sixties and seventies and stretch the roots of the little provincial Mormon community. At the time, I didn't know the town had the look of the other communities in the West settled by Mormons. There was the large and dominating church in the center of town. The farms that surrounded the community were generally without homes. Homes of Mormon villages are in the town where members have easy access to the church. I've read the configuration was first to protect from Indian pillaging—similar to circling the wagons. The home pattern lived on well into the twentieth century. The arrangement facilitated attendance at the many meetings devout members are expected to attend. However, today, like in most Western communities, many of the Saints live in ranchettes beyond the city limits.

The lights of the little town faded in the rearview mirrors that splendid June evening. Our increasing speed cooled the car as the windows went up, and soon, our attention had returned to the radio. "I hear the cottonwoods whisperin' above, Tammy, Tammy." I hummed along. The song with Debbie Reynolds was new that summer. I'll bet we heard that beautiful melody a hundred times those five days and loved it every time. I still know all of the words. Why the state of euphoria? It wasn't the beers. Four of the six were warm in the back seat. The beer survived the trip. Neither of us at that time had acquired a true appreciation for brew. Two hours would put us in Provo.

At about 10:00 p.m., Wayne let off the accelerator, the glass packs crackled and the Pontiac eased into Provo. The air was much warmer than in Vernal. We were down nearly two thousand feet. Unbeknown to us that night, we entered Provo on a main street, University Avenue, and it was still busy with die-hard cruisers. We hadn't passed three stoplights when we detected the silhouetted heads of two girls in the car just ahead.

"Hot damn, Wayne! Let's see if they're friendly."

"Easy now. Don't act too interested."

Twenty minutes later, we were dancing to the Pontiac radio on a junior high school tennis court, the car pulled close to the court's fence. "The breeze from the bayou keeps murmuring low, Tammy, Tammy." It's a waltz, and that was the first of many times I've waltzed to that song. And those girls, whom we assumed to be Mormon, could dance. We would see BYU in the morning. Might even pick up a catalog. The Y was looking good. We backtracked about five miles that night up Provo Canyon to a campground along the Provo River and slept that night, without the girls, I must add.

The next morning, we arrived on the large quad of the BYU campus as classes were changing. Students were going in all directions. They hurried. It was like an anthill just kicked by a big boot. The campus is beautiful. To the east in the near background is the fault-block Wasatch Mountains that dominate the landscape. BYU sits on a terrace of the mountains that rise abruptly less than a mile east of the campus, and that June morning, their peaks were still snow capped. Only along the southwest corner of the campus are there old rock construction buildings.

The most impressive of the new buildings was the Eyring Science Center, and later, I would become very familiar with it. Along with the women, it was the sheer grandeur of the setting that drew us back to enroll. Oh yes, there was Mr. Clark. His influence was considerable. Mr. Clark met us at the Maeser Administration Building where we went to pick up the class catalog. He was an older gentleman with white hair, and he greeted us with a brotherly handshake. We weren't allowed to sit. He escorted us over the campus and took us to the Joseph Smith Building for lunch. Such a burst of friendliness hadn't been the greeting at the Colorado schools. His spirit was infectious. I especially remember his excitement in telling us about the grandiose building plan as we walked about the campus. "The largest university library in the Rocky Mountains will be built over there," he said. "A new student union will be built where those World War II barracks stand."

Back in the Maeser Administration Building, one noticeable use of language between the busy employees told us this place was different. Everyone was addressed as "Brother or Sister." It seemed without exception. "How would that sound, to be called Brother Hansen?"

"Oh, I guess I could adjust, Brother Keown." And that's the way it was back to our homes in Cortez. We addressed each other as "Brother Hansen," and "Brother Keown." Before August, the decision had been made. We would enroll at BYU. But it would be fifteen months later. Wayne went back to Western State. I didn't have enough money to last beyond enrollment.

The summer of 1957 brought me the job with Western Geophysical Company, an oil exploration group, and I was enjoying the work and especially the money. My parents, with three children in college, would be without college funds to support me in the fall. I would work with oil exploration for a year and continue college the following year. It was an extraordinary year of work. For six months, I was on the Navajo Reservation and worked in all of the Four Corners states: Colorado, New Mexico, Utah, and Arizona. I learned first hand the hardships of the Navajos. Some families traveled miles for water in old pickup trucks. There was no electricity. En route to work, our trucks passed Navajo homes, and we crewmembers early in the morning gave candy bars to Indian children at regular stops along the way. Western Geophysical didn't miss a candy bar. Then in December, I was sent to Alaska to work with the first ever helicopter seismograph oil exploration operation. It was rural Alaska as most of Alaska is. People were unassuming, friendly, and helpful. There were few places to spend money. Soon, I could shuffle my paychecks. Later, I would contrast our helpful acceptance by these Alaska pioneers with the difficulties of acceptance of gentiles in the all-Mormon rural communities of Utah.

Finally came BYU. It was September 1958 in Provo and the campus so cursorily examined fifteen months earlier had become Wayne's and my new home. The first Sunday in the afternoon our introduction to LDS theology began with a knock on our basement sleeping room door. It was Rex and Bob, Mormon stake missionaries. They had learned of our gentile status—gentile is common Mormon nomenclature for non-LDS—at the registrar's office. They were there to introduce us to their faith. The two were seasoned missionaries, each having served two-year foreign missions, and I will add, most diligent. Five months later, on Sunday afternoon, the knock of Rex would be expected. Bob quit coming about three months into the undertaking to make us Saints, but Rex continued, though missionaries customarily work in twos.

By spring, Wayne and I had talked many hours with our missionaries. I remember that a lot of the time had been on subjects we did not associate with their goal of converting us to Mormonism. We came to think of them as friends—about our ages with common interests. At their insistence, one Sunday afternoon, we traveled with them to Heber, Utah, about twenty-five miles north and east of Provo, where a couple of Y students from Wyoming were to be baptized at a stake chapel baptismal font. I later learned, with mild embarrassment, that a Mormon stake house or chapel is central to several ward churches. When we entered Heber, a response to a statement by one of the missionaries exposed my naivety about Mormonism. He looked down the block and said, "There's the stake house." I asked, "Are we going to eat first?"

Wayne and I knew the Wyoming guys who were baptized that afternoon. The ceremony didn't persuade us to follow as Rex and Bob hoped it might.

Another meeting we attended was at the insistence of Rex. I recall it being termed a testimony meeting. Members gave testimony about their knowing the Church was true and their belief that Joseph Smith was a true prophet of God who had restored the original Christian Church to the earth. Some of the testifiers, mostly young students, became emotional and were crying by the conclusion of their testimony. I don't recall whether it was following the Heber baptism or the testimony meeting but when Rex came for the Sunday visit, Wayne and I told him we would not be joining the church. I couldn't buy the Joseph Smith story. The missionaries continually admonished us that this could be a crossroads in our lives, and they prayed we would not miss the junction.

I began to get a glimpse of what Rex's life was like in the winter when he told about the monastic existence that he forced himself to endure during that two-year mission in South America. I compared his ordered mission to South America with my chosen voyage to Alaska to earn college money. He was expected to volunteer and was sent by church authorities to go forth and help order the world to LDS thinking and behaving. Rex returned, but there were the unaligned even at his church's BYU. I learned that the church wants to align even those who have long been dead, with the baptizing of the dead ceremonies at the sacred temples. Rex and his associates can't be allowed to relax until the whole human population, past and present, have been shaped in the Mormon mold.

It wasn't your fault, Rex that you failed to convert me or Wayne while you were carrying out your sacred command. I was seeing your society and hearing your leaders. Maybe you were at the regular Wednesday, all-campus religious assembly and heard the puritanical president of BYU, Ernie Wilkinson, relate the parable about leaning on the church for guidance through life's tests of obedience. It was about love and friendship. It had only been a couple nights earlier I had learned about the circumstance from Karen Pota, a girl from Oregon I had come to know. Her girl friend's dilemma was the focal point of Ernie's parable, by my title, "On Friendship." Karen's friend was dating a man who was separated from his wife. Whether there was a divorce pending, I cannot remember. Knowing BYU, sex was not involved. Karen told me that some of the girls were down on their dorm mate and had reported her misbehavior to their bishop. The dorm had become split. Some were in support of her personal freedom to see the man and choose her boyfriends. According to Karen, most of the girls were in support of the girls who had squealed to the bishop, who in turn had summoned the resources of the church to save the sinner. Karen was unquestionably in support of the girl having the freedom to choose her friends, boyfriends included.

That Wednesday before the Y student body, the president's parable was meant to clear the air of any indecision for Mormon children with respect to boy–girl relationships. "The girls who reported to the bishop," he said, "knew the full meaning of the church." Then he addressed the girls who were in support of the sinner. "It is the code of the underworld," he said, "not to be a squealer." To make her bishop aware of the sinful relationship was, according to Ernie, "like calling the fire department at the sign of smoke." Friendship for Ernie was for the girl with her sin to be turned over to the caring arms of the church.

No, Rex, it wasn't your fault. You did your best to bring me into your ordered existence. Was it the degree of freedom in thought and action that my parents had allowed me in my earlier youth? Was it a tolerant and diversified Four Corners Country to grow up in? Maybe it was sympathy for Navajo Indians and hearing them labeled derogatorily by your church as "Lamanites." Or maybe it was that winter, spring, and summer in the free and accepting society of Alaska. It could be that I was just born free. Whatever the cause, in those years when the mind is so flexible, your church's stack of disks that directs about life and every way to turn, so easily transferred to young Mormon children and the uninformed, would not play on the turntable of my mind. So today, Rex, I write on your behalf.

CHAPTER 2

BIRTH IN DARKNESS

Image of statue
of Moroni

Painting of Joseph Smith receiving plates

http://en.wikipedia.org/wiki/Cumorah
New statue of angel Moroni
The angel sits atop Hill Cumorah

Painting by C.C.A.
Chiristensen (1831-1912)
Moroni gives Joseph Smith the
golden plates on Hill Cumorah

*I told the brethren that The Book of Mormon was the most correct of
any book on earth, and the keystone of our religion, and a man would
get nearer to God by abiding by its precepts than by any other book.*

—Joseph Smith
Documentary History of the Church, vol. IV, p.46

DUANE KEOWN

*False facts are highly injurious to the progress of
science, for they often endure long.*
—Charles Darwin

It wasn't over with *The Book of Mormon.* I owed it to the missionaries
Rex and Bob for the hours they carried out their mission, and perhaps
to myself to see if their sacred book was beyond my reasoning. In
Provo, people who appeared content and happy surrounded us. Was I
missing the boat? I would take the test. Many times, the missionaries
admonished Wayne and me that we should personally see if the promise
offered by Moroni in the last chapter of *The Book of Mormon* would
be fulfilled. Before he sealed the scriptures and put the book in the
ground for Joseph Smith to find in the Hill Cumorah centuries later,
Moroni, a final character in the book, wrote in the last chapter what has
become known as the Promise of Moroni. According to Joseph Smith,
thousands of Nephites died in the last great battle with the Lamanites.
The Lamanites won and survived. It was the battle of Armageddon.

But before the massive battle, Moroni, the final scribe of the book, put
down in the gold plates the promise for all following Joseph Smith to
read, and thereby test the veracity of the book. Should the revelation
come to me, it would be a "heart truth," confirmation of a truth with
a feeling, probably not by reasoning or my own investigation. It is a
feeling given to the individual by the Holy Ghost. Mormons know
their American history book is true, because they feel it in their hearts.
It is revealed to them—a warm feeling, a vision . I didn't know what to
expect. But I would test the promise. It is verse 4, in chapter 10, Moroni,
the last chapter of the book.

> And when ye shall receive these things (That is, read *The
> Book of Mormon*), I would exhort you that ye would ask

God, the Eternal Father, in the name of Christ, if these things are not true; and if ye shall ask with a sincere heart, with real intent, having faith in Christ, he will manifest the truth of it unto you, by the power of the Holy Ghost.[3]

It was a Sunday afternoon. I drove my 1948 Chrysler Royal to Utah Lake. On the east shore, a road wound through cottonwood trees and willows and ended above a sandy beach. There in solitude, I could look out across the lake to the western shore and the Lake Mountains. I would do it right. Perhaps, I should have got out of the car and onto my knees. Looking across the lake, I asked the question, "Is *The Book of Mormon* true?" Nothing happened. No pillar of light, the earth did not shake, not even an abnormal breeze. There was no special feeling. Was I not sincere or did I not have real intent? Did I not have enough faith in Jesus Christ? That might have been. Was it my fault? Or perhaps the promise is a catch-22. For those who don't have the great revelation, any abnormal experience or feeling, is it their fault?

For several days, I thought about what I had done that Sunday afternoon. Other than for curiosity sake, I had no special need for what I had done. Why did I need Mormonism? I had considerable success so far in life. I had friends, money in the bank from my year of work in Alaska, and especially, I had a secure wonderful home in Cortez with loving parents. Just maybe, as I suspected, the book isn't true.

It may have been about then in time when I decided on science. A course I was taking, "Comparative Vertebrate Anatomy," really had my attention. Not the course—the instructor was really sub par—so much as the text for the class, *The Vertebrate Body,* by the celebrated biology professor Alfred Romer at Harvard.

My scores were highest on the tests in a class required for premed and pre-dentistry students. For me Romer's book was an eye-opener concerning our own evolution. Romer was keen in investigating vertebrate evolution. Comparing facts from paleontology, comparative anatomy, and embryology, he taught the basic structural and functional changes that happened during the evolution of fishes to primitive terrestrial vertebrates and, from these, to all other tetrapods, humans included. He always emphasized the evolutionary significance of the relationship between the form and function of animals and the environment: gill arches to chin bones, air bladders to lungs. Through the course, I asked myself if the instructor, Dr. William Banner, understood the full meaning of Romer's text. He could not or would not relate the significance of the author's message to us humans and our evolution.

Today, knowing the thin academic ice BYU professors play upon, especially the biologists, Banner's role in the curriculum in the 1950s is better understood. Romer strengthened my faith in science and human evolutionary history, which seemed diametrically opposed to the religious-centered life surrounding us that relied upon the supernatural.

The scientific method and processes, in use for two hundred years since the first Mormon prophet's revelation, have given us the evidence that Smith's history book has no relevance to the record produced by archaeology, genetics, and other indicators used by serious scholars. Why and how did the millions of LDS living, and the millions who came before, get swallowed up into Smith's "divine history"? It alters their every waking moment. Their first identity becomes, "I am Mormon."

There is probably a direct correlation between a population's belief in answers to phenomena and relationships in the universe and its understanding of the processes of science. Their answers may seem irrational to scientists. Not only in Utah, but also all over the United States, students can complete the high school science curriculum and never engage in science as a verb. The general science class, chemistry class, or the biology class is often about facts, what scientists contributed to the knowledge base of science, rather than the processes that allowed the scientists to make their discoveries.

This shortcoming of science education is not a characteristic of U.S. science teaching alone, though our students rank embarrassingly low internationally in science. Where myths and folklore reign to explain nature, science knowledge and its processes are poorly understood or respected. That Joseph Smith would have learned the story of the history of the peopling of the Americas from golden plates buried in the Hill Cumorah in New York, and that an angel delivered these detailed records to him, is the principal event that amasses millions of Mormons. The event is contrary to and a revocation of the process of science. In claiming Mormon scriptures to be the word of God, they become absolutes.

In science, there are no absolutes, only realms of certainty. Based upon belief in Joseph Smith's story, millions of human hours are spent, and have been spent, trying to persuade the world to fall in line and forfeit lifetimes of human energy. Countless hours rely upon an event that is contrary to the way science or history acquires knowledge. In a long conversation with the late Dr. Sterling McMurrin, a famous student of Mormonism, he told me personally, "History books are not written that way." McMurrin was a professor of philosophy and history at the

University of Utah and President Kennedy's Secretary of Education, before there was a Department of Education.

Joseph Smith and Charles Darwin were contemporaries, born only four years apart. To understand the legitimacy of knowledge, it is most useful in our time, to compare the lives of the two men. Their avenues to what they considered knowledge were very contrary, and to understand the routes, it is necessary to recapture the environments where the two men spent their lives.

First, let us look at the time and locale of Joseph Smith. He was born in Sharon, Vermont, in 1805, four years before Darwin. Smith's ancestors had lived in New England for a hundred years but never in the relative luxury of the founding fathers. Within New England, Sharon, Vermont, was frontier country at the end of the eighteenth century. Vermont was the last of the original thirteen colonies to be admitted as a state to the Union and had been a state for less than eight months when the Smith's arrived.

The stage upon which the Mormon Church was born is less than two hundred years old, and the mood and complexion of American life and thought in the location of his birth are well documented. Life at the foot of the Green Mountains was full of hardships. Most people were poor, indelicate, and seriously unschooled. Joseph's mother could read and, late in life, wrote an autobiography that revealed herself as a deeply religious person.

With the winning of political independence from England, thousands of

New England families also declared independence from the established European religious denominations. Religious freedom was hammered into or lived on in the constitutions of every New England state following the Revolution, except for those professing to be atheists or agnostics. In many of the state constitutions, statements such as this one in the Arkansas constitution lasted well into the nineteenth century: "Article 19, Section 1: No person who denies the being of a God shall hold any office in the civil departments of this State, nor be competent to testify as a witness in any Court."

The Smith family starved out in Vermont. With their eight children, when Joseph was ten years old, they moved farther west to Palmyra, New York. There were common schools in the area, and in the nearby town of Manchester, there was a library that boasted of six hundred volumes. But later, when Joseph Jr. attempted to write about his visions and revelations, his grammar, spelling, word usage, and especially his intellectual poverty, revealed a man who was poorly educated. He was unaware, at least in his early manhood, of the great intellectual movements astir in his day.

The American and French revolutions had had repercussions that were felt throughout the world, among the rich, the poor, the educated, and the uneducated. Old political systems and religious codes were cracking, and schisms were developing. But nowhere was there such unfettered religious liberty as on the American frontier. The frontier was not only where a man or woman could escape the shackles of the European economic status quo, but he or she could be religious, or not, or even start a religion of his or her own.

On the frontier, in Joseph Smith's time, there began the Shakers, four brands of Methodists, Free-Will Baptists, Hard Shell Baptists, and the Foot Washers, to name a few. Only twenty-five miles from Joseph's home, there was Jemima Wilkinson who was known as the "Universal Friend." She governed her following with revelations, as Joseph would later do, and she swore that she would never die.

In none of the writings of Joseph Smith was the scientific approach to the acquisition of truth and knowledge about the universe advanced. He was out of the mainstream of American and European intellectual life and the advancing disciplines of science. In the backwash, his search for truth and knowledge was a short-cut method. He merely asked God.

What was the nature of Smith's divine meetings and revelations from God? His first revelation came when he was fourteen, according to his unpublished autobiography. He said, "I was seized by some power that entirely overcame me." He was asking God in prayer which church in the area to join. "I was answered that I must join none of them, for they were all wrong, and the personage who addressed me said that all their creeds were an abomination to His sight…"[4] (*History of the Church,* vol. III, p. 29, publication of the LDS Church). The second important meeting of Joseph with angels came the night of September 21, 1823. He didn't write about the encounter until 1838 when he was writing the official history of the establishment of the church, but he was able to describe the experience in detail. He wrote that he was kneeling by his bed in a shabby room asking for forgiveness of his sins. A light filled the room, and a person appeared and stood in the air beside him.

> He had on a loose robe of most exquisite whiteness…
> His hands were naked and his arms also, a little above
> the wrist, so, also were his feet naked, as were his legs,
> a little above the ankles. His head and neck were also

bare... his whole person was glorious beyond description, and his countenance truly like lightning.

He called me by name and said unto me that he was a messenger sent from the presence of God to me and that his name was Moroni; that God had a work for me to do; and that my name would be had for good and evil among all nations, kindreds, and tongues, of that it should be both good and evil spoken of among all people. He said there was a book deposited, written upon gold plates, giving an account of the former inhabitants of this continent, and the sources from whence they sprang. He also said that the fullness of the everlasting Gospel was contained in it, as delivered by the Savior to the ancient inhabitants; also that there were two stones in silver bows—and these stones, fastened to a breastplate, constituted what is called the Urim and Thummim—deposited with the plates; and the possession and use of these stones were what constituted "Seers" in ancient or former times; and that God had prepared them for the purpose of translating the book.[5] (*No Man Knows My History*, Fawn Brodie, p. 39, Alfred A. Knopf, 1945. And, lds.org/scriptures/pgp/js-h/1.30-32?lang=eng#29 [LDS website])

Joseph said he did find the plates at the Hill Cumorah, which by now is a holy shrine to Mormons the world over. Joseph said that the plates were not immediately given to him nor was he allowed to touch them. It was required by God that he visit the site once each year for the next four years during which time he would be sufficiently purified. On September 27, 1827, he said that he took the plates home, but his family was not allowed to see the plates. In 1828, Joseph Smith did not have the literary skills to write *The Book of Mormon*. His wife Emma became his first scribe, followed by a neighbor farmer, Martin Harris, and finally, Oliver Cowdery.

Smith so intimidated the scribes concerning their fate if they were to see the golden leafs, that the entire work was dictated to the scribes without their ever viewing the plates. Oliver Cowdery witnessed that he saw them after they were translated. Joseph sat on one side of a partitioning curtain while his scribes sat on the other and recorded. Thus were created the roots of the Mormon faith. Joseph Smith gave birth to a new religion, and its growth continues, although the paper documents laid out at its founding have been eroded and are unbelievable to skeptics of the supernatural today. It wasn't unwavering belief in the plates but the character of Joseph Smith, the condition of his followers, and the ripeness of times that spawned the new religion on the frontier.

The plates revealed to Joseph that American Indians were descendants of the Lost Tribe of Israel, a conclusion that was readily accepted by most clergymen in Europe and America at that time. It was a conclusion hoped for and very plausible in the minds of the European discoverers of America. For devout Christians, to find evidence that might link the American Indians with events of the Bible was what they wanted to hear. For most Europeans and Americans of the time, the Bible was an accurate history of earth; hell was beneath the feet for the unworthy, and heaven was above for the righteous.

Only two years before Neil Armstrong set his feet in the dust of the moon, in the forests of the southern Philippine Islands, a small tribe of aboriginal people were discovered who were still building fires with the heat from the friction of twisting a wooden stick against another larger stick[6] (*National Geographic Magazine*, August 1972, p. 219). The Tasaday tribe was twentieth-century Stone Age people without a written language. In 1967, they were unaware that in a world outside their tribal forest, a larger society was preparing for a landing on the moon. Such a disparity in human accomplishment and awareness of the universe was shocking and almost unbelievable in the second half of the twentieth century. Only through rare circumstances of isolation could such an ancestral time in human advancement have been preserved. Today there is controversy whether the Tasaday tribe was actually as Stone Age as first reported. But certainly they were far from being in touch with mainstream 20th Century technology and happenings.

In 1969, when it was announced, "the Eagle has landed," it was immediately common knowledge throughout the world. By contrast, it was a very different world inherited by Joseph Smith and Charles Darwin with respect to communication. International news in the first half of the nineteenth century was still carried by boat. There were several tribes, like the Tasadays, to be discovered. No man can be faulted for his condition of birth, not the Tasadays of the Philippines, the underprivileged Navajos on their southwestern U.S. reservation, nor Joseph Smith in Sharon, Vermont, in 1805. We are heirs to a rich cultural and intellectual heritage, the victims of our parents' location and impoverishment, or somewhere in between. But did Joseph Smith believe his own story? The question could have only been answered by the first prophet.

Throughout history, the great centers of human awareness and advancement have developed where there have been the greatest numbers of links for the worldwide gathering of information. Throughout the eighteenth and nineteenth centuries, England—London in particular—had no equal as a world center for gathering and synthesizing current knowledge about the planet and the cosmos. England was linked to the outreaches of the world through colonies and trade. As the sun didn't set on the British Empire, neither did the lanterns go out in the British universities and colleges. The only advantage to learning about the known world and the universe greater than living in the London area would have been to be born wealthy with time to use the educational resources of the British society. That was the inheritance of Charles Robert Darwin.

February 12, 1809, was not an ordinary day for the political or intellectual fortunes of the world, for on that day Abraham Lincoln was born in America and in Shrewsbury, England, Charles Darwin was born. In Sharon, Vermont, Joseph Smith was four years old. Charles Darwin's father was a three-hundred-pound medical doctor who had married Susannah Wedgewood, an heiress to the international Wedgewood Ceramics business, the makers of Wedgewood china. Susannah died when her son, Charles, was only eight. His father never remarried.

For the Darwin and Wedgewood children, success by the traditional English standards was assumed. Erasmus Darwin, Charles's grandfather, was a well-known natural philosopher in England whose book *Zoonomia* was read by the natural scientists of Europe. Erasmus was a keen observer of the living world; he had been counted among the first describers of ecological relationships between organisms. In a very disciplined but loving and humane home, Dr. Robert Darwin set very high standards of accomplishment and created a rich environment for intellectual, social, and financial success. He was a tireless practitioner of medicine and enjoyed a reputation as an excellent diagnostician of diseases. Throughout his entire life, Charles was in the most nourishing intellectual surroundings offered by the nineteenth century. At the "Mount," as Dr. Darwin's home was called, the library contained hundreds of books. Distinguished professors, business leaders, and political leaders were frequent guests.

Though not considered a precocious child, Charles was recognized as a close observer of his environment. As a youth, he spent an unusual amount of time in collecting what must have been to him the oddities of nature: insects, worms, shells, fossils, etc. In his early schooling, he was bored by the characteristic teaching styles of the period: memorization and recitation.

In October 1825, at age sixteen, Charles Darwin entered Edinburgh College, intending to become a medical doctor. He seemed a natural; congenial and readily liked. It was probably his father's choosing. In his second year, Charles observed surgery at the medical school. Anesthesia in surgery was still several years away. Midway through the operation, Charles left the viewing gallery. Shortly after, he announced to his father that it was not his desire to become a physician.

In 1828, Charles enrolled at Cambridge to become a clergyman in the Church of England. He successfully completed the requirements and received the BA degree from Christ's College in 1831, without honors. Though he never entered the clergy, his decision to join the Cambridge academic environment was one of three profound decisions that set the course for his life study and changed the way we view our relationship to life on our planet. At Cambridge, Darwin immediately made friendships with several professors who were leaders in their academic fields. These were friendships that lasted his lifetime. It was almost as though Darwin was singled out for the special qualities they saw he possessed. By the time he was twenty-two, he had become an insatiable reader. He remained at Christ's College, intent on becoming a clergyman and someday having his own parish. But his courses in natural science brought him to the forefront of thought and theory in several fields of science. By the age of twenty-two, Charles had added to his unique powers of observation the other requisites for true scientific accomplishment: discipline of thought and an uncompromising desire for reported facts.

As luck favors the prepared mind, luck may also catalyze its fruition. It was luck at age twenty-two that brought Darwin the great opportunity that led him to unsought-after fame and for the rest of humankind a documented thesis describing the origin of the staggering variety of life on earth. It was because of a recommendation by his professor friend H. S. Henslow that Charles was accepted to be the naturalist aboard the HMS *Beagle*. The British government commissioned the voyage. Scheduled to last three years, it was a scientific voyage, one of the first of its kind. The objective was to explore the Southern Hemisphere. Charles' assignment was simply "to collect and observe anything new." For Darwin, acceptance of the position and the assignment was the second profound decision he made that would lead him on to a lifetime quest to explain the processes that govern the natural world.

In America, only a year prior to the voyage, Joseph Smith, with some supporters, published *The Book of Mormon*. It contained answers to questions about the North and South American continents including their inhabitants. Smith's book was quickly written compared to science and history books, but its writings didn't require research. His was a book of revelations that dealt in science topics; time would test its thesis as time has the habit of doing in areas that are open to scientific inquiry. While Charles Darwin was preparing to add to the great legacy of scientific understanding, Joseph Smith was answering the burning questions concerning the environment he was encountering.

Smith's approach was very different. It was a compendious method that would yield quick, but poorly conceived answers. The answers would only be acceptable to persons as naïve as Joseph about the natural processes of our biosphere. Unlike Darwin's supposition, Joseph's theses would need no proof, for he would claim a divine relationship in its deliverance. In his claim, he would gain the power and respect that had not been bequeathed to him by the condition of his birth or his own intellectual accomplishment.

When the HMS *Beagle* began the voyage, Darwin was by no means an accomplished naturalist. Among the men who chose the crew, it was respect for Darwin's potential, his energy and likeable character that instilled confidence in their selection. By the time the ship sailed, December 27, 1831, the voyager had sought out the most recent and reliable description of the world he was about to visit. He read the publications his professional friends supplied him concerning diverse viewpoints about the origin of landforms and life forms. It was almost as though his associates sensed the great reward the voyage would produce. Darwin was about to undertake a journey that would lead him to the earth's great showcases of geological and biological processes— the Andes, coral reefs, Galapagos Islands, Australia, and Africa. He had combined the rich intellectual cultures of England and his family heritage with his unusual powers of observation, energy and genius. He was ready. Darwin stood upon the shoulders of the geologists Charles Leyell, Adam Sedgwick, and James Hutton; the biologists Jean Lamark,

H. S. Henslow, his grandfather Erasmus, and hundreds of other scholars who had elevated him to his condition of understanding.

The Book of Mormon was translated, according to Joseph, from golden plates by using the magical Urim and Thummim stones given to him by an angel of God. In about three months, Joseph translated from the plates to his scribes "the true history of the aboriginal people of North and South America." The book had no references, but it needed none. Its contents were not based on observations of any living man, not even Joseph Smith. For Mormons, it is a work of God through Joseph Smith. But it was born in a vacuum, and as nature abhors a vacuum, so does science abhor and invalidate the illogical and unfounded thesis.

By contrast, Darwin's *The Origin of Species Through Natural Selection* was the culminating document following a lifetime of observation and research by a man who had unusual opportunities. By the time Charles Darwin began writing his classic book, his mind was a vast resource about the natural world we live in. He had sailed around the world on a voyage that lasted five years, instead of the planned three years. He walked and rode horseback many hundreds of miles in many countries, encircling the earth, collecting specimens, and taking notes concerning his observations. His notes on the Beagle voyage alone numbered eight hundred handwritten pages. When he returned, there subsequently followed years of reading scientific journals. Before he began writing his theory of evolution, he was an internationally known naturalist. He had the money and the time to dedicate to his studies, his family, and his closest friends, who were mainly scientists. Charles's ideas were freely exchanged with his closest science friends.

Darwin taught us to observe. I recently retraced Charles Darwin's steps in the Galapagos Islands, the trails he took in September and October of 1835. He was twenty-six years old, and it was the fourth year of the voyage of the Beagle. He recognized the volcanic birth of the islands and the geological newness of the archipelago relative to South America. He saw the similarities and differences of Galapagos species to those of the South American mainland, six hundred miles to the east. He noted the differences in mocking birds, finches, and the giant tortoises on each of the four islands he visited during his five-week exploration. But it wasn't until 1859, twenty-four years latter, that he published his theory of the origin of species. It followed years of investigations that convinced him and his scientist associates that in isolation, groups of a species can deviate from the original species, and in time, no longer belong to the original species.

During the same time period that Darwin was recording his observations of South America and contrasting the species of South America and the Galapagos archipelago, Joseph Smith was in a different world with his new church organization in Kirtland, Ohio. The members were completing the Kirtland Temple. Revelations were coming to Joseph regularly from God about the organization, administration, and even construction of churches and temples. From 1835 to early 1838, the Latter-day Saint population of Kirtland more than doubled, from about nine hundred to two thousand[7] (*The Heavens Resound: A History of the Latter-day Saints in Ohio, 1830–1838*, Milton V. Backman Jr., p. 140, Deseret Books 1983).

In September 1835, the first edition of *Doctrine and Covenants*, which is holy gospel for the church, was published. The first publication contained 102 early revelations from God to church leaders, mainly Joseph Smith Jr. and his companion through the church's beginnings,

Oliver Cowdery. Today, the *Doctrine and Covenants* contains 138 sections, or revelations, and two Official Declarations, also believed to be revelations from God. The first 135 sections contain Joseph Smith's revelations from 1823 to 1844. Declaration No. 1 is dated 1890 and is referred to as "The Manifesto" which declared an end to the practice of polygamy. Declaration No. 2 is dated 1978 and declared that "all worthy male members" could now hold the priesthood and participate in the temple ceremonies. This ended the LDS Church priesthood ban on Negroes. Belief in their scripture books as the word of God lives on and governs the lives of modern LDS. In May 1987 in the *Ensign,* an official publication of the LDS Church, the thirteenth president and prophet of the Mormon Church, Ezra Taft Benson (1985–1994), said about the relationship of *The Book of Mormon* and *Doctrine and Covenants:*

> Excluding the witnesses to the *Book of Mormon,* the *Doctrine and Covenants* is by far the greatest external witness and evidence which we have from the Lord that the *Book of Mormon* is true. At least thirteen sections in the *Doctrine and Covenants* give us confirming knowledge and divine witness that the *Book of Mormon* is the word of God (see D&C 1; D&C 3; D&C 5; D&C 8; D&C 10–11; D&C 17–18; D&C 20; D&C 27; D&C 42; D&C 84; D&C 135). The *Doctrine and Covenants* is the binding link between the *Book of Mormon* and the continuing work of the Restoration (of the original Christian Church) through the Prophet Joseph Smith and his successors. In the *Doctrine and Covenants* we learn of temple work, eternal families, the degrees of glory, Church organization, and many other great truths of the Restoration.[8] ("*The Book of Mormon*—Keystone of Our Religion," Ezra Taft Benson, *Ensign,* November 1986, p. 4)

Revelations (Sections) cited by Benson in *Doctrine and Covenants* are those of God to Joseph Smith telling Smith that his *The Book of Mormon* is true. Is this a source of reference—Smith for Smith?

In teaching biology in southern Utah's Mormon-dominated schools never did I neglect Darwin's contribution to our biological science knowledge. Nor did I contrast his acquisition of knowledge to Joseph Smith's method. His way of knowing was their way of knowing. However, my predecessor as the biology teacher in the Monticello High School was Mormon and told me before he left the high school about students walking out when he broached the evolution subject. His rapport with the students was poor on his good days and probably the reason I took his place.

Charles Darwin had been exposed to some thinking about evolution before embarking aboard HMS *Beagle*. So a popular conception that Darwin's voyage gave him the idea of evolution is not accurate. Yet is it true that the years of travel and research focused Darwin's mind and sharpened the powers of observation that would eventually lead to the publication of *On the Origin of Species*. In 1838, Darwin read the Rev. Thomas Malthus's Essay on the Principle of Population (1798). Malthus had argued for a law-like relationship between population growth and food production in order to warn against what he feared was an imminent danger of overpopulation. Malthus was widely believed to have conclusively demonstrated that population would necessarily outstrip food production unless population growth were somehow checked. This focused idea inspired Darwin who applied it to his much wider field of concern. Darwin, already concentrating on how new varieties of life might be formed, now thought in terms of the differences between those individuals who, for whatever reasons, left offspring and those who did not.

Darwin began keeping notes on the subject of the transmutability of species in 1833. His search for a theory how species could change included correspondence and visits with animal breeders. He also carried out experiments to test the survival of seeds in salt water, wondering about the plausibility of seeds being transported to new volcanic islands across the oceans from the continents. In all, several volumes of notes accumulated that would substantiate a theory. Unlike the revelation of *The Book of Mormon* and *Doctrine and Covenants* that started with the answers, Darwin looked for the evidence and a theory that his evidence would support. His was a true work of science.

Darwin knew well the dissention that the publication of his findings would cause. After all, he trained to become a minister in one of England's finest theological colleges. In his orthodox Christian society, even in his own family, his findings ran counter to the biblical story of creation, and he was hesitant to publish. His science friends with whom he shared his views encouraged him to publish. He began writing *The Origin of Species* in the summer of 1855. For more than twenty years, he had collected the evidence.

Perhaps he decided to publish when he became aware that across the world in Borneo, Alfred Wallace, who was in grade school when Darwin began work on his theory, was onto the same idea. On June 18, 1858, Darwin received a parcel from Wallace, who was working in Malaysia. It enclosed a letter and a twenty-page manuscript for an article describing an evolutionary mechanism, with a request to send it on to Charles Lyell if Darwin thought it worthwhile. The article, titled "On the Tendency of Varieties to Depart Indefinitely from the Original Type," contained the same conclusions concerning the processes of evolution that Charles had spent half a lifetime documenting. The two men had previously communicated with each other about the problem, but research has shown that they both came upon the same conclusions independently[9] (*Darwin's Century,* Loren Eisley, pp. 291–292, Doubleday 1958).

Charles Lyell and Joseph Hooker knew how long Darwin had toiled in developing and demonstrating his theory. They approached the Linnean Society, and it was agreed that articles by Darwin and Wallace would be read at the same July meeting of the Linnean Society in 1858. Darwin soon followed with his book, *The Origin of Species Through Natural Selection,* documenting his theory with the observations and facts he had recorded over three decades. The work was printed in November of 1859. Time has honored the book. One hundred and fifty years after the first printing, it remains a best seller in science writing. It is a monument to the methods of science.

The theory of evolution is today the framework upon which modern biological science is built. Even to the Christian fundamentalists, and others who continue to oppose evolutionary theory, there is a practical acceptance. Loren Eisley, the late eminent anthropologist, describes how important the theory is to all of us in our everyday lives: "Even those who loathe the very names of Wallace and Darwin today seek out unquestioningly, when ill, doctors whose whole medical experiments are based upon the fact that one form of life is related to another"[9] (*Darwin's Century,* Loren Eisley, p. 292, Doubleday 1958, cited previously).

By contrast, *The Book of Mormon* is the antithesis of *The Origin of Species.* It lives by faith alone; faith in a history told by one man to his friends and relatives. Time has been its enemy. The Smithsonian Institution is an international source for the knowledge acquired by science and science research. In 1996, the following was the prepared statement given to those who inquired about scientific evidence for the Mormon history of the Americas.

1. The Smithsonian Institution has never used the *Book of Mormon* in any way as a scientific guide. Smithsonian archeologists see no direct connection between the archeology of the New World and the subject matter of the book.

2. The physical type of the American Indian is basically Mongoloid, being most closely related to that of the peoples of eastern, central, and northeastern Asia. Archeological evidence indicates that the ancestors of the present Indians came into the New World—probably over a land bridge known to have existed in the Bering Strait region during the last Ice Age—in a continuing series of small migrations beginning about 25,000 to 35,000 years ago.

3. Present evidence indicates that the first people to reach this continent from the East were the Norsemen who briefly visited the northeastern part of North America around AD 1000 and then settled in Greenland. There is nothing to show that they reached Mexico or Central America.

4. One of the main lines of evidence supporting the scientific finding that contacts with the Old World, if indeed they occurred at all, were of very little significance for the development of American Indian civilizations, is the fact that none of the principal Old World domesticated food plants or animals (except the

dog) occurred in the New World in pre-Columbian times. American Indians had no wheat, barley, oats, millet, rice, cattle, pigs, chickens, horses, donkeys, and camels before 1492. (Camels and horses were in the Americas, along with the bison, mammoth, and mastodon, but all these animals became extinct around 10,000 BC at the time when the early big game hunters spread across the Americas.)

5. Iron, steel, glass, and silk were not used in the New World before 1492 (except for the occasional use of unsmelted meteoric iron). Native copper was worked in various locations in pre-Columbian times, but true metallurgy was limited to southern Mexico and the Andean region, where it's occurrence in late prehistoric times involved gold, silver, copper, and their alloys, but not iron.

6. There is a possibility that the spread of cultural traits across the Pacific to Mesoamerica and the northwestern coast of South America began several hundred years before the Christian era. However, any such inter-hemispheric contacts appear to have been the results of accidental voyages originating in eastern and southern Asia. It is by no means certain that such contacts occurred; certainly, there were no contacts with the ancient Egyptians, Hebrews, or other peoples of Western Asian [sic] and the Near East.

7. No reputable Egyptologist or other specialist on Old World archeology, and no expert on New World prehistory, has discovered or confirmed any relationship between archeological remains in Mexico and archeological remains in Egypt.

8. Reports of findings of ancient Egyptian, Hebrew,

and other Old World writings in the New World in pre-Columbian contexts have frequently appeared in newspapers, magazines and sensational books. None of these claims has stood up to examination by reputable scholars. No inscriptions using Old World forms of writing have been shown to have occurred in any part of the Americas before 1492 except for a few Norse rune stones, which have been found in Greenland.

9. There are copies of the Book of Mormon in the library of Natural History, Smithsonian Institution.

Mormon archeologists protested to the Smithsonian Institution, but not with their evidence to counter the statements above. It was for the reason that the institution is administered and funded by the government of the United States. It is separated from religion by the constitution. In the article, "New Light: Smithsonian Statement on the Book of Mormon Revisited," in the *Journal of Book of Mormon Studies*, volume 7, issue 1, p. 77 (1998), the author explains,[10] "More recently members of Congress have questioned the Smithsonian Institution about the inappropriateness of a government agency taking a stand regarding a religious book." In March of this year (1998), the director of communications at the Smithsonian began using the following brief response to queries about *The Book of Mormon:*

> Your recent inquiry concerning the Smithsonian Institution's alleged use of *The Book of Mormon* as a scientific guide has been received in the Office of Communications. *The Book of Mormon* is a religious document and not a scientific guide. The Smithsonian Institution has never used it in archeological research and any information that you have received to the contrary is incorrect.

But *The Book of Mormon* is more than just an undocumented story and a book of faith, for it is not harmless. Seven times in the book, groups of people who have sinned are cursed with dark skin. It fosters a very primitive and racially abusive belief in cursed peoples who are descendants of sinners and, therefore, must regain stature in the eyes of their God. It is a stifling, racist belief without foundation in biological science or human history. Yet in 2009, the formal missionary program for the church is responsible for sending out over fifty-six thousand missionaries to approximately 330 organized missions around the world spreading Joseph Smith's revelations. For the missionaries, their faith conquers reason. It is heart truth. And for children, stories from the book are printed and appear on the World Wide Web propagating unfounded and anger-provoking history.

What happens to the individual who buys into the first prophet's story and converts to the faith? If the Mormon follows the protocol of the church to progress toward the celestial kingdom in heaven, there is a life of sacrifices. There is a two-year mission to disperse the story and recruit converts, temple rituals to go through that are earned by living the LDS described righteous life, receiving the garments and then wearing them throughout the rest of life, observing the Word of Wisdom (no alcoholic beverages, tobacco, coffee, or tea), paying one-tenth of one's income to the church, and the list goes on. So many sacrifices are made and rules are followed that the Saint's first identity becomes, "I am a Mormon." It is a life based on faith that Joseph Smith's story is true. A while back, I read a bumper sticker on a Mormon family car that affirmed the naiveté, obedience, and the reliance on faith by those who buy the story. It said, "Discover America, read *The Book of Mormon*."

CHAPTER 3

THEY REALLY BELIEVE
THAT STUFF

This sketch is similar in idea to a painting of dark skinned "Lamanites" published by the LDS Church and was on the World Wide Web in 2011 with Book of Mormon Stories for children (lds.org/media-library/video/book-of-mormon-stories?lang=eng&start=1&end=12). It's caption stated, "Laman and Lemuel's followers called themselves Lamanites. They became a dark-skinned people. God cursed them because of their wickedness."

The First Curse of the Lamanites (American Indians) from *The Book of Mormon*:

2 Nephi 5:20–21

Wherefore, the word of the Lord was fulfilled which he spake unto me, saying that: Inasmuch as they will not hearken unto thy words they shall be cut off from the presence of the Lord. And behold, they were cut off from his presence.

And he had caused the cursing to come unto them, yea, even a sore cursing, because of their iniquity. For behold, they had hardened their hearts against him, that they had become like unto a flint; wherefore, as they were white, and exceedingly fair and delightsome, that they might not be enticing unto my people the Lord God did cause a skin of blackness to come upon them.

It was raining that October 1968 evening in Spanish Fork, Utah, when my Mormon friend Garry Dailey, his wife Peggy, and I stopped my Toyota Crown sedan in front of the home where Garry's father-in-law and mother-in-law lived. Years had passed since BYU days, but life continued for me in Utah after a couple of interludes. I was in my fourth year teaching biology, and other sciences, at Monticello High School. Monticello is in southeastern Utah, a twenty-minute drive from the Colorado border. The picturesque little town at the foot of the Abaho Mountains is about 90 percent Mormon, but traditional LDS life and its foundations are moderated some by its proximity to Colorado. Some of the gentile Colorado pinto bean and wheat farmers trade in Monticello, and a few send their children to Monticello schools. A main transportation artery from the Four Corners Country to Salt Lake City runs through Monticello.

Throughout my time in Monticello I was aware the LDS Church still covertly ran Utah, especially southern Utah. My family and I knew the motions that rocked the boat, and generally, we did not make them. Moderation with alcohol, abstinence from tobacco and holding middle class values, perhaps even skewed to the conservative viewpoint, allowed the family to move with the flow. After all, my father had for many years been a Republican county treasurer in Dolores County, Colorado, and during the depression in the 1930s, my grandfather Gage was the Republican sheriff of the county. The county bordered Utah to the west. In Monticello, it was commonly known that I was a BYU graduate. and most of the community probably believed I was a "Jack Mormon," one of those who would shun the rigid LDS behaviors but want to be buried by the Saints. In fact, by 1968, I had acquired a somewhat accommodating attitude and had been successful at education in Utah. In 1971, with my teaching career complete at Monticello High School, I was in graduate school at Ball State University in Indiana. The graduating Monticello High School seniors called me back to give the commencement address.

The occasion in October that brought us to Spanish Fork that rainy evening was a meeting of the Utah Education Association in Salt Lake. Spanish Fork was a short diversion from the route to Salt Lake City. Garry was the local school district teacher's association president, and I was the president-elect. As we left the car and rushed through the rain to the cover of the in-law's carport, the elderly, happy mother and father hugged their daughter and her husband and gave me a friendly handshake. I sensed the abundant affection for each other and their admiration for Garry. For a Mormon son-in-law what more could they have wanted? He was a loving father and loyal to his family. He abounded with energy for his church and teaching public school—one year, he was named Utah Teacher of the Year—and he carried out a ranching operation on the side. To people who remarked about how much he accomplished he would say, "Everyone gets twenty-four." He knew his religion. He served a two-year mission in Sweden and was immediately liked by everyone he met. And he remains my good friend.

As sure as I knew the rain would stop, I knew what the interior of the home would be like. Peggy's parents were devout Mormons, and we were in heartland Utah. The little home would have served for the LDS model. Very visible in the living room were the gospels of the church, works the members believe were divinely inspired: *The Book of Mormon, The Bible, Doctrine and Covenants, Word of Wisdom*, and the *Pearl of Great Price*. Devoutness for many Mormon families seems to be measured by their familiarity with the church's divine publications. My BYU experience told me that some secular work is shunned and others critically slighted, anthropology in particular. When I attended BYU, a sign on the road announcing the entrance to the campus read, "The Glory of God is Intelligence." The adage still is in large letters on the cover of the Brigham Young University Graduate School catalog.

As the meal was about to begin, the elderly mother turned to me and asked, "Are you a member?" I didn't ask, "Of what?"

"No," I said. It did not set me back. For many older Saints it was an oft-asked question of a suspect, especially in the heartland. Of course, there was grace. After a wholesome supper of soup, Garry, his father-in-law, and I retired to the living room. The chair that I sat in was closest to the kitchen door. Peggy and her mother talked about family, and I could hear them, as we males carried on light conversation. Our male conversation has long been forgotten, but a comment I overheard from the kitchen remains in my mind and is primary to my reason for writing these pages. Peggy said to her mother, "Mom, you know what Lyle (her youngest son) told me the other night before he went to sleep? He said he knew the church is true." Lyle at that time was seven or eight years old. This was "Mormon heart truth," as the author of *Losing a Lost Tribe*, Simon G. Sutherton, might refer to it. It is true because it is true in the heart. It was a beautiful proclamation to Peggy, and I am sure it was consoling to the grandmother. It may have been bliss for the mothers, but for me and for the outer society that Lyle might engage, it was an ominous sign of future intellectual and social conflict with the gentile world and other religions.

By high school, Mormon children, if they have the proper LDS upbringing, are convinced that theirs is God's only true church. I realized this one night as I drove a school bus with Monticello High School students from Carbondale, Utah, to Monticello. The value of a teacher to a small high school is directly proportional to the variety of duties he or she can or will perform. There is hall duty, lunch duty, ticket-taking, prom supervision, bus loading… the list goes on.

So it was for me that late and cloudless night I was driving the Monticello High School Pep Club across the barren landscape of southeastern Utah. The high school basketball team had just defeated East Carbon High. Our victory over that impoverished school was commonplace in those years. East Carbon was at Sunnyside, Utah, a small isolated gentile town with many Catholics in Mormon-dominated Utah. It existed for the sole purpose of getting the coal out of the ground for Geneva Steel, the large foundry near Provo, and to keep lights glowing in Salt Lake, a hundred and fifty miles to the north.

Monticello High's cheerleaders occupied the seats immediately behind me at the front of the bus. As we left the school gym, the customary yelling and screaming resonated from the bus windows to announce to the small town's residents that Monticello was victorious. The razzing was met with unfriendly reminders that Monticello was a Mormon town. One boy walking from the gym flipped his lighted cigarette at the bus to note his nonobservance of the Mormon Word of Wisdom. Another kid gave us his raised middle finger. As the excitement of our boisterous exit diminished, conversations drifted back to the usual teenage stuff; who is going with whom, who is about to break up, pop music, the topics of teenagers. But for the students immediately behind me, the talk reflected upon the behaviors of the gentile students who signaled, as we departed, differences between the Monticello kids—actually their religious community—and the people of Sunnyside.

The conversation began with denouncements of the gentile ways. "Did you see that kid flip his cigarette at the bus?" asked one of the girls. "Yes, and I could smell beer everywhere in that gym," said one of the most respected of the cheerleaders, daughter of a school administrator. One by one, the most superficial factors that separate Mormons from the gentiles surfaced. Finally, Lynne Donan defined the basic gentile problem. The Sunnyside kids didn't have the gospel. Without the revelation of the Word of Wisdom through Joseph Smith, how were the people of Sunnyside to know the sins of tobacco and alcohol, or the crudeness of the middle finger sign?

With her definition of the problem, there was peace of mind with the children in the conversation at the front of the bus—with all but one, the gentile student John Crider. "I don't smoke or drink," he said. "In fact, no one in my family does. We don't have your gospel either." John's statement produced a silence. But I knew it wasn't because he had provoked thought about why some people smoke and others do not. It was because he questioned the gospel as the power that guided their behavior.

As our school bus rolled across the southern Utah desert, the thought came to me how content and satisfied these children were with their behaviors. Unswerving faith in their gospel and their leaders had held them together through the persecutions in the Midwest. It was their common belief in their destiny that had seen them through the hardship of settlement in the unpredictable Rocky Mountains. With the same kind of reasoning, with gratitude for their divine doctrine, the Mormon children reasoned why they had defeated East Carbon, why they didn't smoke or raise their middle finger at their opponents. Once again, they had been rewarded for living the revealed message. Like the tribes of Old Israel and the Nephites in the Americas, they would prosper in the land because they were righteous.

In a real sense, it was good that the children didn't smoke and were respectful of each other and refrained from signaling with the middle finger. I often asked myself, why question the motivation for virtuous behavior. They live that way.

After completing the doctorate degree at Ball State University with a full-ride scholarship from the National Science Foundation, the superintendent of San Juan School District asked me to become the first principal at the San Juan Junior High School in Blanding, Utah. The junior high grades had been part of the high school in the old high school building, and it remained part of the newer high school complex.

"Duane, you get along better with those people than I do," I remember him saying, as we met to consider the position. He was speaking of the Navajo parents and their students. He was remembering my experience several years before, when I had taught on the Navajo Reservation in the San Juan School District. I had taught at Aneth, Utah. It was the second time teaching in the district with a provisional elementary teaching certificate. I had just finished college at BYU, and it remained difficult to hire teachers for the outreaches of San Juan County, Utah. But the county was the highest paying district in the state, and I was offered a bonus to teach on the desolate Navajo reservation. I was broke again after completing the Bachelor of Science degree at BYU in zoology. My assignment was two elementary grades, and I also drove the school bus.

"They don't participate in the activities, except the rodeo team," the superintendent continued about Indian students in Blanding schools. "There are more Navajos than whites in the Blanding high school now. Not one Indian boy is on the high school football team or basketball team. The Indians all sit grouped together in the classrooms. They want their own high schools down on the reservation. See what you can do." I said I would and became the principal.

Early on at the junior high, I became close friends of the brothers Charlie and Jim Landy. They were Navajo teacher aides for the junior high grades, and immediately, I found they were my able liaisons with the Navajo students and families whose language I could not speak. But even better than that, the brothers knew basketball and wrestling. They had both been high school stars.

Prior to becoming the principal, during the five years I taught science in the Monticello High School twenty miles to the north, I had come to know the school integration problems of Blanding. Some of the Indian students in the Junior High and High School grades were bussed more than fifty miles one way to Blanding. The wealth of San Juan County gave Monticello and Blanding beautiful new schools. But the location of the wealth was in the south end of the county on the Navajo reservation. Most of the large Aneth Oil Field was in the Utah corner of the Four Corners Country. El Paso Gas Company at Aneth was the county's largest taxpayer. The Navajos were pushing for their own high schools. Blanding stores were being painted with AIM (American Indian Movement) graffiti, and serious measures needed to be taken to promote harmony. The superintendent said the schools and Blanding needed me.

It was during my second year as principal of the San Juan Junior High School, 1973–1974, that a group of Anglo Mormon parents requested a meeting with me about playing time for their boys on the basketball team. The meeting was in the evening at the school. "We really feel sorry for the Lamanite children and their lives, but Charlie Landy is not being fair," said Mrs. Bekins, spokeslady for the parents. "He isn't letting our boys play enough." Early on, when I learned how Charlie Landy played basketball I appointed him to coach the basketball team. "He is like all coaches," I explained. "He wants to win. He is playing the kids he believes are his best players." And he was winning. In fact, he was beating the Anglo Mormon schools to the north of Blanding; Monticello, Moab, and others. When I became the principal, the coach had been an Anglo Mormon, and the Indian students had not joined the school for basketball. Now, they were the basketball first team. Charlie's brother, Jim, was the wrestling coach. Some of his wrestlers were Indians, and they were winning too. I consoled the parents. I said

I would ask Charlie to see that the Anglo kids got more playing time. After all, it was junior high school.

But my lasting carryover from the basketball meeting was not the playing time of the Mormon boys but that in the public school meeting when Mormon parents would talk about the "Lamanite" students. Seven times in their God-given book, God curses the Americans Indians with dark skins. They are the descendants of wicked Laman. Back home that evening, I told my wife, Betty, about the Lamanite labeling of the Indian boys by the Blanding parents. "They really believe that stuff," she said. She knew, having grown up in a gentile family in Monticello. In her youth, the dominant church in town was the LDS church. All of her friends were Mormon. She joined. When I met her while teaching at Aneth, she had left the Saints, though her name was still on the roll.

Why had the labeling of the school's American Indian students as Lamanites angered me so? At BYU, "Lamanite" was academic. Had it not been for my experiences and friendships with Navajos, perhaps I would have shrugged off the Mormon classifying of these people. I thought about Charlie and Jim Landy who had become close friends. We shared aspirations for the Navajo and Ute students of our school. But more importantly, we had become friends, like Bob Thompson, Garry Dailey, and even Wayne Hansen.

I reflected on the poor Navajo children that came onto the school bus I drove at Aneth on the reservation. Out of their hogans without electricity and after sleeping on the dirt floor, they would board the bus. The only flush toilet some had ever seen was at the school. It was cruel enough that Anglo Americans put them on reservations to eke out an existence in the hostile desert, but to call them Lamanites? And to believe they were descendants of a sinner so evil that his offspring would be cursed with black hair and dark skin hit a raw nerve with me. It was the Saints who saw dark hair and skin as a curse, and it was from Joseph Smith. I didn't just dislike for them to be called Lamanites, I hated the label, and the biological ignorance that the idea lived in.

You may recall, I started this book back in the 1980s soon after the move from Utah to the University of Wyoming. I didn't return to the task until retirement, officially in 2003 and unofficially in 2009. It was the fall of 1984. I was on sabbatical leave in Salt Lake City where I had all of the resources about Mormons and their history. The plan was to complete two articles for science education journals begun earlier and commence research for the book about my experiences with Mormons during the Utah years. Perhaps the book should begin with an excursion into the thinking of Utah children was my thought one morning while on the University of Utah campus. After all, I taught those children for ten years before the move to UW. How would I sample their thinking about such issues as cause of skin color, Old Testament beliefs that are unrealistic today but reincarnated by Joseph Smith? I would need to ask students. It would be quite easy. My doctorate was in biology education, and I was on sabbatical leave for a year. A year-long sabbatical leave only allowed me to draw half pay, unlike a six-month leave wherein I could draw full pay. As a substitute science teacher, I would receive pay, which I could sure use, and ask the questions of Utah students. I could examine beliefs that may affect students' acceptance of modern facts and theories concerning natural science and history, especially as it relates to humans.

To survey the beliefs of secondary-school-age students, I became a substitute teacher in the Granite School District, Utah's largest. Approximately 50 percent of students of Salt Lake City are Mormons. I volunteered to substitute in all classes and at all secondary schools of the district so that my survey would be random throughout the district. My brief anonymous questionnaire was given to 508 students at Granger High School, Brockbank Junior High, and West Lake Junior High School. I constructed a Likert-type scale with response categories from 1, representing "No, I strongly do not believe the concept," to 5, meaning "Yes, I do strongly believe the concept." Response summaries to the questionnaire are shown below. The study and commentary was published in the July/August 1986 issue of the *Humanist,* "What Utah Children Believe," pp. 21–26.[11]

What I Believe and Don't Believe

1. There are still miracles or supernatural happenings going on all of the time, like in times of old.

1	2	3	4	5
10.10%	16.7%	25.15%	22.18%	29.9%

Total % 1+2 = 22.77%   Total % 4+5 = 52.08%   Mean% = 3.49

2. Earth was created in six days like it says in the Bible.

1	2	3	4	5
12.96%	6.09%	17.88%	11.98%	51.08%

Total % 1+2 = 19.05%   Total % 4+5 = 63.06%   Mean% = 3.86

3. There was a flood in the time of Noah, and Noah built a large boat or ark that enabled earth's life to survive.

1	2	3	4	5
5.98%	5.60%	12.36%	18.53%	57.53%

Total % 1+2 = 11.58%   Total % 4+5 = 77.56%   Mean% = 4.16

4. Adam and Eve were the first humans on earth. They lived in the Garden of Eden which was a perfect environment like the Bible says.

1	2	3	4	5
7. 59%	7.39%	14.40%	13.42%	57.20%

Total % 1+2 = 14.98%   Total % 4+5 =70.62%   Mean% = 4.06

5. Sin on earth began with Adam and Eve breaking God's commandment to not eat the forbidden fruit.

1	2	3	4	5
10.41%	5.30%	18.27%	12.97%	40.67%

Total % 1+2 = 15.71%   Total % 4+5 =53.64%   Mean% = 3.93

6. There is a devil on earth, and he causes people to do bad things.

1	2	3	4	5
14.79%	9.73%	16.34%	12.45%	46.67%

Total % 1+2 = 24.51   Total % 4+5 = 59.14%   Mean% = 3.67

7. God may sometimes cause curses on people when they become sinful.

1	2	3	4	5
39.73%	14.29%	24.27%	11.54%	10.18%

Total % 1+2 = 54.02%   Total % 4+5 =21.72%   Mean% = 2.38

8. In ancient times, God cursed American Indians and blacks with dark skin. In time, the curse may go away.

1	2	3	4	5
56.06%	9.82%	18.30%	7.71%	8.09%

Total % 1+2 = 65.88%   Total % 4+5 = 15.80%   Mean% = 2.02

9. I believe that humans evolved on this planet from lower forms of live.

1	2	3	4	5
35.03%	10.65%	29.78%	7.50%	16.77%

Total % 1+2 = 45.95%   Total % 4+5 = 24.27%   Mean% = 2.60

10. I believe the idea of overpopulation in Utah is a bunch of bunk. Utah can provide for the people that are born here.

1	2	3	4	5
10.59%	8.24%	30.39%	19.22%	31.57%

Total % 1+2 = 18.83%   Total % 4+5 = 50.77%   Mean% = 3.53

Keep in mind the results of the survey were from metropolitan and suburban Salt Lake City students. What might the results have been in rural communities where the school-age population of Saints was greater than 95 percent?

On December 4, 1984, I met with Donald La Feurre, spokesman for the LDS Church, and asked him if Saints are still expected by their leaders to believe that races of humankind have been cursed with dark skin. He said, "Yes, God's ways are not man's ways." I asked him if he foresaw any changes in these Mormon scriptures that seem so unscientific and socially inappropriate in the twentieth century. He replied, "No. The Saints must take these explanations by faith."

The survey is expository concerning our society's advance beyond the Saint's gospel. The knowledge of schoolchildren has gone beyond Smith's explanation for human racial differences. It is reassuring. Yet, the grown men, the authorities of the church, must be true to Smith's revelations and say to members and the public that they believe the first prophet's explanations that came through God's revelation.

Seventy-seven percent of the secondary students believed literally in Noah's flood, and nearly that many, 70.62 percent, believed that Adam and Eve were the first humans and lived in the perfect environment of the Garden of Eden. There is social support for belief in these concepts among Mormons. Since 50 percent of the Salt Lake City population is gentiles, there is an assumption that about half of the gentile children who completed the survey believed in Adam and Eve as the first humans and Noah's Ark. But as the survey indicated, only the most orthodox fundamentalist Mormons cling to the idea that dark-skinned people are cursed. One such orthodox Mormon boy surfaced as the questionnaires were being handed in at West Lake Junior High School. I was standing at the back of a geography class as the students were handing their completed surveys to me. Two eighth-grade boys, one Anglo and one black, had just returned to their desks that adjoined one another in the same row. The little black boy whispered to the white boy, "What did you put on that one about curses on Indians and blacks?" In an embarrassed and almost apologetic voice, the little white boy answered, "I put they're cursed. But we believe someday the curse will go away." The little black boy shook his head.

Of the religious beliefs surveyed, I was least surprised about the students' belief in Noah's flood. Maybe this was because I realized how little biology most students and their parents know about the relationships of earth's life forms and ecosystems. I'll go back to a class I took as an undergraduate at BYU called "science and religion." At BYU, each student who registers for a semester—it was the quarter system while I attended—must take a course in religion. First, I took religion for non-Mormons, and then followed a search for religion classes wherein I might not have to hear over and over about Joseph Smith's revelations, the substance of the LDS gospel. I looked for courses such as world religions and science and religion. I wasn't about to run out.

Dr. Henry Nichols was a well-known human physiologist on the BYU faculty and leader in the LDS sphere. In the spring semester, he offered the class, Science and Religion. He was especially respected by the young LDS. He was an authoritative scientist, and as I learned later in the semester, made an extreme effort to make science compatible with the students' "heart truths."

Each religion class at the Y began with a prayer. Usually, the professor would ask a student to lead the prayer. Mormon students were comfortable in leading a prayer to ask for the Lord's guidance through the class. I was always nervous, but was never asked. In Dr. Nichol's class, I was new to and inexperienced in biology but I won't forget the class period when Dr. Nichols dealt with Noah's ark. He probably felt obligated to endorse the flood because Joseph Smith linked Noah's rescue of all of earth's life inescapably with the Saints' theology. I left the class that day with my head spinning and asking where the science was in the science and religion course.

Joseph Smith carved the story into stone, and again and again, Church prophets and authorities have etched the story deeper and deeper. It is the poster child of the faith versus science conundrum, not only for the LDS faithful, but also for all Christian fundamentalists. For a devout Mormon biologist at BYU, it is an ecological and physiological nightmare, a "heart truth" they are expected to acknowledge—should they be asked by an LDS Church authority or a BYU administrator. Certainly, who would deny the flood to a class of Mormon students? Dr. Nichols spent the class period trying to make the flood scientifically acceptable, a task impossible without resorting to the supernatural.

I remember he said that Noah might have taken a male and female of one species to represent a whole genus, not necessarily two of every species. He said that might have allowed the seed of all life to fit onto the ark with its space limitations. And since the time of the flood, he said each genus might have given rise to the millions of species that exist today. This was in 1960, one hundred and one years after the publication of Darwin's *Origin of Species*. Had he read the Bible and considered the time element?

I remember how silent the class was after his explanation, including myself. Today, I know how thin the ice is for biology teachers in Utah, as well as the Bible heartland of the United States, to make the scientific stand on Noah's flood or organic evolution. In southern Utah, I became acquainted with biology teachers who tiptoed over evolution and the flood in fear their jobs would be in jeopardy. Had they really taught the biology, it would be an honorable way to lose a job, like John Scopes in "The Monkey Trial." According to the Old Testament, we are looking at six thousand years of mankind. Species evolve in hundreds of thousands or even millions of years. If I were in Dr. Nichol's class today, I would ask him to read a single article that appeared in a rather obscure journal, *Creation/Evolution,* the winter issue, 1983. It was titled, "The Impossible Voyage of Noah's Ark" by Robert Moore.[12]

Joseph Smith in his revelations confirmed the flood of Noah's time. With the dark skin races, Smith inadvertently was treading into modern genetics. But with Noah's ark, Smith was dabbling into animal physiology, plant and animal ecology, animal behavior, geology, geography, and the engineering of shipbuilding, just to get started. First, let's look at how the flood and creationism are woven into Mormon scriptures and how the flood is dated with the prophet Smith's chronology. The scripture below is from *Doctrine and Covenants* (Smith revelations) 84:14–17.

> Abraham received the priesthood from Melchizedek, who received it through the lineage of his father even till Noah; And from Noah till Enoch, through the lineage of their father; and from Enoch to Abel, who was slain by the conspiracy of his brother, who received the priesthood by the commandments of God by the hand of his father Adam, who was the first man... Which priesthood continueth in the church of God in all generations, and is without beginning of days of end or years.[13]

Adam is not only the first human, but he is given a time. Just follow his lineage to Abraham, about six thousand years. Of course Mormons and fundamentalist Christians can say that each descendant lived for millions of years. Joseph Smith had an opportunity to change the chronology. During the years 1830–1833, he revised the King James Version of the Bible. With struggles against neighbors in Nauvoo, Illinois and the murder of Joseph Smith, the main body of Saints left Illinois for Utah with Brigham Young. What became the Reorganized

Church of Jesus Christ of Latter-day Saints remained at Nauvoo. They had the only copy of Smith's revised Bible, *The Holy Scriptures*. Smith's revision leaves the flood intact, and for both the Utah Mormons and the Reorganized Church, the flood is official scripture. Smith's rendition of the flood adds very little that is new to the story, but the fact that he claimed his revision to be modern revelation, less than two hundred years ago, increased the difficulty for Saints to view the story allegorically as do other Christians of this century. Smith reaffirmed the story. Again, it was hot off of the press. Here are a few essential elements of the story as revealed to Joseph. These scriptures are all from the book of Genesis in *The Holy Scriptures*.

> And God said to Noah, the end of all flesh is come before me; for the earth is filled with violence, and behold, I will destroy all flesh from off the earth.

> Make thee therefore an ark of gopher wood; rooms shalt you make in the ark and thou shalt pitch it within and without with pitch; and the length of the ark thou shalt make three hundred cubits; the breadth of it fifty cubits and the height of it thirty cubits. And behold, I even I will bring in a flood of water upon the earth, to destroy all flesh, wherein is the breath of life, from under heaven; everything that liveth on the earth shall die. And thou shall come into the ark, thou and thy sons, and thy wife, and thy son's wives with them. And of every living thing of all flesh, two of every kind shalt thou bring into the ark, to keep alive with thee; they shall be male and female.

> And the waters prevailed exceedingly upon the face of the earth, and all the high hills, under the whole heaven were covered. Fifteen cubits and upward did the water

> prevail; and the mountains were covered. And all flesh died that moved upon the face of the earth...
>
> And Noah only remained, and they that were with him in the ark. And it came to pass, in the six hundred and first year, in the first month, the first day of the month, the waters were dried up from off the earth. And Noah went forth, and his sons, and his wife, and his son's wives with him. And every beast, every creeping thing, and every fowl upon the earth, after their kinds went forth out of the ark.

Joseph Smith had a literal belief in the story of the flood. He referred to the flood in *The Book of Mormon*, Alma 10:22, Nephi 22:9, Ether 6:4; *Doctrine and Covenants,* Sec. 84:14–15; *Pearl of Great Price*, Moses 7:43, 20:23–24. The attention that Mormons give to the Genesis version of Creation and Noah's saving each kind of life has unwittingly placed them in the camp of the fundamentalist Christians and creationists, and with little respect from the scientific community.

Creationists, with their newest banner of intelligent design, start out with sure answers and proceed backwards looking for evidence, the reverse of the scientific method. Scientists even try to falsify the best logic to know the truth[14] (Popperian Idea, *The Logic of Scientific Discovery*, Karl Popper, 1959). To reverse the influence on the public and its demise on science by creationists, there is a rather impassioned campaign by the scientific community, even into the courts. Court battles have placed late twentieth and twenty-first century science in the ring with authoritarian beliefs of a long gone era. Creationists have never won in court.

With "The Impossible Voyage of Noah's Ark," the author, Robert

Moore, takes the creationists almost as seriously as they take themselves. I will summarize his article. I hope you find the article entertaining and informative with side benefits about seafaring, botany, zoology, ecology, zoo keeping, and shipbuilding. Let me quote from Moore's beginning.

> Suppose you picked up the newspaper tomorrow morning and were startled to see headlines announcing the discovery of a large ship high on the snowy slopes of Mt. Ararat in eastern Turkey. As you hurriedly scanned the article, you learned that a team from the Institute for Creation Research had unearthed the vessel, and their measurements and studies had determined that it perfectly matched the description of Noah's ark given in the book of Genesis. Would this be proof at last—the "smoking gun" as it were"—that the earliest chapters of the Bible were true and that the story they told of a six-day creation and a universal flood was a sober, scientific account? Perhaps surprisingly, no.

And Moore continues. What may have been believable in the mind of the early Hebrew is today the completely impossible. First, we will look at the state of shipbuilding in the time of Noah's voyage. For the old gentleman to have built a boat 450 × 75 × 50 feet—the English measurement equivalent of cubits given in the Bible—around 4000 BC would have been comparable to the Wright brothers building the space shuttle.

The technology of any industry must develop. Many relics of ships belonging to the ancient sailors of the Mediterranean region have been found and give a rather accurate chronology of the development of the naval industry. From Egyptian history, we know the length of a cubit, and the ark was about three times longer than any ship being constructed at the time, and many times larger. While the state of the art was reed boats and hollow logs, Noah was building the equivalent of a twentieth-century freighter. A floating structure the size of the ark was not built until the late nineteenth century, and then it was built of steel. The largest wooden ships ever constructed were about three hundred feet in length. They were built in the early twentieth century, and the nature of wood for such a large vessel was completely impractical and was the reason that shipbuilders turned to steel. The largest of the wooden ships were reinforced with steel, yet they leaked profusely due to the bending of the wooden beams, and they could be seen undulating as they moved through the water. Several hundred shipbuilders were used to build boats of this size—Noah had a crew of eight, and he still had time to roam the country and preach of doomsday, and beg his neighbors to repent. Noah was a very able man.

As Robert Moore puts it, "Noah's boat-building accomplishments have not been fully appreciated by his fans." Perhaps equally distressing, what happened to the ship building technology that Noah's family must have developed? According to Genesis, his family returned to an agrarian life. The world waited six thousand more years before a ship near the size or with the success of the ark was engineered. But construction of a ship with the requirements of the ark was a minor problem compared to the biological difficulties of the feat.

Joseph Smith's inspired translation of Genesis stated that all flesh of the earth would be destroyed except two of each kind that are not clean and by pairs of seven of each kind that are clean. His translation didn't distinguish which organisms are clean and which ones are not clean. To biologists, a "kind" of organism that would be taken on the ark would have to be a species. By definition, a species is a group of organisms that naturally interbreed. For example, a zebra and a donkey are not of the same species since in nature they are not known to interbreed, although in captivity successful reproduction has taken place. This would mean that to replenish the earth with its diverse kinds when the voyage ended, a bare minimum of 1.9 million species must have filed off the boat.

The acclaimed biologist E. O. Wilson says that we may not have discovered even a third of earth's species. There are more than nine hundred thousand species of insects. In the single class Insecta of the phylum Arthropoda, there are seven thousand to ten thousand new species reported each year. Our 1.9 million minimum number of species includes only two hundred thousand species to represent the fossil kinds. Remember, all the fossil kinds must be on the ark too, since the incident was only a few generations removed from the creation of the first life. To sincere Mormon believers and creationists, the fossils in the rocks are the remnants of the life destroyed in the flood and now buried in the sediments deposited on the bottom of the seas when the cataclysm ended. Let's read on.

Moore determined that with a very liberal count there would be 3,858,920 individuals on the boat. There would be 1,687,500 cubic feet of space in the boat for the precious cargo. There would be 0.437 cubic feet per occupant. Even a pond snail needs a gallon of water. For the larger aquatic animals, the problem becomes even more difficult. A tank at Marineland of the Pacific contains four small whales and some dolphins, and it is eighty feet in diameter and twenty-two feet deep. It contains 640,000 gallons of water. The largest whales, which are not in captivity, would require a tank the size of a football stadium. The blue whale is believed to be the largest animal ever to live on the planet, including the brontosaurus, a couple of which would also be on the vessel.

The largest blue whale ever recorded was 110 feet long and weighed 172 metric tons[15] (www.wikipedia.org/wiki/Largest_organisms).

But if the boat were built, it had to be loaded. Noah's mission only becomes more impossible. Moore asks, "Does the polar bear one morning have a premonition that the Arctic is to be flooded and head south for the Mediterranean coast? Does he ignore his favorite food, the seal, as they wait patiently in the line for the day of boarding?" The cave animals pose a special problem. They are without pigment in their skin, and many of them do not have functional eyes. How do they find the ark? The sessile animals of the oceans and lakes, the corals, sponges, sea anemones, have no way of transporting themselves across continents to the big boat. Noah had to get the plants aboard too. Some seeds will not live a year and some do not reproduce with seeds. And there were piranhas, alligators, grizzly bears, and even bumblebees to coax into the ark.

All of the organisms were loaded in one day, including Noah's family. From Joseph Smith's Bible we read, "In the selfsame day entered Noah, and Shem and Ham, and Japheth, the sons of Noah, and Noah's wife, and the three wives of his sons with them." Moore determined that in order to load the nearly four million individual organisms within the biblical timetable of one day, 44.6 of them went up the gangplank every second!

And how did the disease organisms board the boat? Many organisms are hosts to parasites that cannot live without their specific hosts. Humans, too, are hosts for many obligate parasites, most of whom affect us as diseases. And there are the symbiotic commensals, those organisms such as *E. coli* bacteria in our large intestines that cannot live without us, or we without them. All of these critters had to escape the flood, too, and there was only one location where they could have survived—on and in Noah's extended family. There were eight in the group: Noah, his wife, their three sons, and their wives. Moore lists the organisms that are host-specific to humans: five types of bacterial venereal disease organisms, four species of malarial parasites, three species of lice, one pin worm, a tapeworm, three agents of filariasis, and two species of the genus, *Schistsoma*, blood flukes. Now we really begin to appreciate the family of the ark, as Moore describes them: "These eight unfortunate souls were afflicted with enough diseases and discomforts to support a hospital—all in their part in preserving life through the great flood."

If the barge had floated, would the cargo have replenished the earth? For many species, reproduction is not accomplished with just two, even if both are fertile, which may have had limited probability with two million pairs. Some birds will only mate when they are in flocks. Individually, or even in pairs, some bees and wasps will not survive.

If there had been room for food and fresh water aboard the ark, the eight crewmembers would have been especially busy. Nearly all of the animals needed special diets: panda bears need bamboo shoots; monkeys, fresh fruit. A large elephant eats several hundred pounds of hay per day and gets sores if it is unable to bathe. Even in the twenty-first century, some animals' needs are so specific—they are so dependent on their natural environment—we have not yet learned to keep them in zoos.

When the flood ended and the time came for unloading the weary passengers, the ark was stranded high upon the side of Mt. Ararat in eastern Turkey. From atop the mountain, the journey back to their homes began for the plants and animals—the kangaroos to Australia, the tapirs across the ocean to South America, and the fish from the deepest oceans depths back to their habitat.

By the way, how were those organisms from the greatest depths of the ocean kept on the ark? They require great water pressure. When brought to the surface they die. In the millions of years of evolution, the lives of species of organisms have become intricately woven into the fabric of the ecosystem that sustains all members. It is child's thinking to believe that the survivors of the flood would return to the drowned, desolate rotting communities of their origin to "start over." There would have only been miles of barren sediment filled with the decaying matter that had been only a few generations before declared "perfect"—that is the Genesis story.

And where did all that water come from, and where did all that water go? Mt. Everest is five miles high, and it has organisms near its summit that would have survived had it not been immersed. Ninety-seven percent of the earth's water is in the oceans, and the shorelines tell us that they are today essentially where they were at the supposed time of the flood, less than six thousand years ago. It is obvious that if all of the continental water was to run into the oceans and the ice caps were to melt, there would not be enough of a sea level rise to even flood Florida, our flattest state. It would rise less than five hundred feet. And if there were three times more water on earth, enough to cover the tops of the tallest mountains, where did the water go when the flood was over? That is a lot of water to hide, even with God's intervention.

There are realistic Mormons who see the uselessness of the creationists' position—the total lack of evidence—and they scoff at the suggestion of Mormon alignment with creationist fundamentalism. But how can they deny the universal flood that destroyed "all flesh from off the earth?" It is basic to their revealed theology. To refuse the flood is to refuse the important element of the prophet Joseph Smith's teachings. He confirmed the catastrophe repeatedly. Consequently, the most believing of Latter-day Saints join with their late apostle Mark E. Petersen when he tells them:

> The flood was a miracle. The episode of the animals and other life taken aboard the ark was another miracle. The rise of the waters out of the depths of the earth and the downpour from the skies were God's doing. And so was the subsequent receding of the waters. The deluge covered the earth and the waters receded just as God planned it all. And it truly was a miracle.[16] (*Noah and the Flood,* p. 65, Deseret Books, 1982)

Suspension of biophysical law is the only "rational" response. I have heard the Mormon and Christian fundamentalist answer to the biblical flood. "If God created the earth, he can cause a universal flood." We can't answer that. But we can ask the question, "Why would God do that?" Most of the organisms had never seen man, even if our species had become wicked. Why would God create the peaceful gorilla, the docile koala bear, meadows of flowers, the mighty elephants, innocent babes, and then summarily drown them? He left not a trace of evidence.

Believers in the flood are in two groups. They do not understand the biological and physical impossibility, or through faith, they believe in the supernatural. To believe in the supernatural is to believe anything can happen. But it is not for those in science to mock the believers in the flood. We point out the impossibility, and the believers are who they are. Jeff Lockwood tells me, "Old Testament Yahweh was an angry, vengeful deity. Love and mercy seem to be on his son's agenda."

Joseph Smith said that the plates were not immediately given to him nor was he allowed to touch them. It was required by God that he visit the site once each year for the next four years during which time he would be sufficiently purified. On September 27, 1827, Joseph said that he took the plates home. Joseph told his family that he received the plates at the Hill Cumorah, which by now is a holy shrine to Mormons world over. It is in western New York and officially recognized by the authorities of the LDS church as the site of the recovery of the golden plates from which *The Book of Mormon* was produced. According to Smith, it is also where two great American civilizations were destroyed, the Jaredites in about 600 BC and the Nephites in about AD 400. Joseph said the Hill Cumorah and others like it were built by the Nephites for fortification. Geology says different.

The Hill Cumorah is a drumlin, a structure caused by the draining of the continental glacier that covered most of New York during the Ice Age. There are hundreds of them in the drainage path of the glacier that covered New York about twenty-one thousand years ago. They are big mounds of glacial debris and sediment. In 1827, what did Joseph Smith know about the Ice Age in New York? Or for that matter, what geological sites did geologists of the early nineteenth century link with the Ice Age?

Joseph Smith could sell Hill Cumorah as a Nephite fortification to the uneducated and the educated alike in the 1820s. By doing the math of *The Book of Mormon*, perhaps two million Jaredites and nearly three hundred thousand Nephites died near the Hill Cumorah. Wouldn't remnants of the two great battles have been found there? Since there have been no steel swords or armaments of any kind found at the New York site and they are talked about in *The Book of Mormon,* many Mormons believe the Hill Cumorah may be somewhere else, perhaps in Central America.

For more than fifteen years best-selling author and historian Hampton Sides has traveled widely across the continent exploring the America that lurks just behind the scrim of our mainstream culture. Reporting for *Outside,* the *New Yorker,* and NPR, among other national media, the award-winning journalist has established a reputation not only as a wry observer of the contemporary American scene but also as one of our more inventive and versatile practitioners of narrative nonfiction.

In the spring 1999 edition for *Double Take Magazine,* Sides wrote the article "This is Not the Place" and focused his attention on the Mormon summer drama that draws loyal Saints from the world-over to celebrate Smith's recovery of the golden plates. It begins, "Near the town of Palmyra, New York, rising over cornfields and dairy farms and the dark green thread of the Erie Canal, is a glacial formed monadnock known as the Hill Cumorah. It's too small to qualify as a mountain, but in its context, Cumorah is an arresting sight, wildly out of scale with the somnolent farm country. At the hill's summit is an American flag, an asphalt pathway lined with pink rosebushes, and a golden statue of the Angel Moroni, from *The Book of Mormon.*"[17]

Hampton Sides attended the Hill Cumorah Pageant, the largest outdoor play in America, in 1998. Sponsored by the LDS Church for seven nights each summer, its cast is over six hundred Mormons and has an audience of nearly ten thousand nightly for seven nights. They sit on the grass and watch the drama depicting the divine deliverance of the golden plates to Joseph Smith by the angel Moroni. The story ends with the battle of the Lamanites and Nephites on the Hill Cumorah. Moroni is the only Nephite survivor, and he buries the golden plate history of the Nephites and Lamanites in the hill for divinely chosen Joseph Smith to find fourteen hundred years later.

The archeological quandary is what happened to the remains of the Nephites and the Lamanites, who according to the Mormon traditionalist, died in the thousands at the Mormon shrine. There has not been a trace found of the thousands of warriors. Is this another miracle? According to *The Book of Mormon*, they used steel swords, they had chariots, and they had horses, cows, and pigs, all from their Egyptian beginnings. Mormon archaeologists have never made a serious attempt to find artifacts from the gigantic battles waged near the Hill Cumorah. The last battle would have been waged about fourteen hundred years ago, near the zenith of the Anasazi culture—the mesa top dweller age—of the Four Corners Country in Southwestern United States.

Literally, tons of Anasazi artifacts have been found. In the region of Blanding, Utah, many skeletons of these American Indians had been discovered by the Mormons. What really happened at the Hill Cumorah, and why haven't the Mormon archeologists excavated to find the remnants of the great Nephite civilizations that met their everlasting there? Don't the LDS church authorities owe it to the members to explore the area and prove or disprove this culminating event in the Nephite civilization, once and for all? Or do they again appeal for a miracle.

The whole area around the drumlin has been farmed for nearly two hundred years, and it has yet to produce a single artifact linking the area to *The Book of Mormon* story. Sides posed the critical problem for Mormonism, "What happens when the ground refuses to cooperate, when the soil fails to yield what the faith insists is there?" Even Mormon archeologists understand that upon the land that was the habitat for thousands upon thousands of Nephites and Lamanites, fourteen-hundred-year-old artifacts should be strewn all over. Mormon archeologists have never begun the digging for the fear of the embarrassment or even the loss of the faithful by not being able to substantiate the Joseph Smith story.

Besides that, the geographical descriptions of the Saint's primary scripture book do not fit the New York area, or any other area of the American continents for that matter. Did these people not leave the Mediterranean with chariots, European farm animals, steel, an alphabet, a language, and technology that never caught on with the New World's Native Americans? American Indians did not use the wheel for practical purposes. *The Book of Mormon* did not fit a cold climate, and there were no "narrow necks of land," in the New York region.

Native American cultures of Central America fit better with a sophisticated people such as 1000 BC Egyptians. For seventy years, Mormons have searched Mesoamerica for ruins and evidence of Middle Easterners. With success in finding evidence of these people, it would cause the world to take note, and at least establish some credibility for the history given the nineteenth century by the prophet Smith.

In the 1950s, BYU archeology turned especially to Guatemala, Honduras, and parts of the Mexican states of Veracruz, Tabasco, Oaxaca, and Chiapas for another Hill Cumorah. But in sixty years of searching, and with the most professionally respected methods and reporting, the ground has not tied *The Book of Mormon* and the Hebrews to the American continents. There have been millions spent and untold hours of toil in digging and screening for the evidence.

Thomas Ferguson is the godfather of Mormon archeology. He was a devout Mormon attorney who retired in the early 1950s from the FBI and was determined to tie Smith's book of revelations to the land, as Smith said would happen. In a letter to Mormon President/Prophet David O. McKay, dated December 14, 1951, Ferguson wrote, "If the anticipated evidences confirming the Book of Mormon are found, worldwide notice will be given to the restored gospel through *The Book of Mormon.*"

Ferguson was a promoter. He persuaded well-off Mormons to finance the archaeological endeavors beginning in 1952. He even persuaded the hotel magnate J. Willard Marriott to accompany him on a trip to the Promised Land. He organized the New World Archaeological Foundation (NWAF). So the professionals would not claim Mormon bias in the relationship of artifacts to the Mormon's holy book, Ferguson hired several renowned non-Mormon archaeologists to help carry out the exploration.

The zeal of the retired attorney to validate *The Book of Mormon* did not enter the scholarship of the NWAF. Over the years, the foundation developed an international reputation for professional work. Gareth Lowe, a Mormon archaeologist, served for thirty years as the foundation's director. But sadly, at the close of his career, Hampton Sides asked Lowe if he still was a faithful Mormon, and he replied, "Well, my wife still is"[12] ("This is Not the Place," Hampton Sides, *Double Take Magazine*, Spring, 1999, cited earlier).

In 1975, Tom Ferguson wrote a twenty-nine-page paper titled "Written Symposium on *Book of Mormon* Geography." He listed the plants, animals, and artifacts mentioned in *The Book of Mormon* that had not been found. His list went, "Ass: None, Bull: None, Calf: None, Cow: None, Goat: None, Horse: None, Ox: None, Sheep: None, Sow: None, Elephant; None." Ferguson went on with the list of *The Book of Mormon* particulars not found: barley, figs, grapes, wheat, bellows, brass, breastplates, chains, iron, mining ore, plowshares, silver, metal swords, metal hilts, engravings, steel, carriages, carts, chariots, glass. The evidence for their existence in pre-Columbian Mesoamerica was "zero." Ferguson's conclusion was, "With all of our great efforts, it cannot be established factually that anyone, from Joseph Smith to the present day, has put his finger on a single point of terrain that was a *Book of Mormon* geographical place." (Taken from "Written Symposium on *Book of Mormon* Geography" in "This is not the Place" cited previously)

Michael Coe, perhaps the most eminent Mesoamerican archaeologist in the twentieth century and professor emeritus at Yale University, worked with the NWAF scholars in the fifties, sixties, and seventies and comes down even more bluntly on *The Book of Mormon* as a historical document. He credits the Mormon archaeologists with doing good work and avoiding pressure from many Mormons to find something to authenticate the Mormon faith. Coe states:

> The bare facts of the matter are that nothing, absolutely nothing, has ever shown up in New World excavation which would suggest to a dispassionate observer that *The Book of Mormon,* as claimed by Joseph Smith, is a historical document relating to the history of immigrants to our hemisphere.[18] (www.irr.org/mit/bom-arch-v1. html#Endnote%2021)

In August 25, 1984, Dr. Raymond Matheny, a former BYU professor of anthropology, spoke at a Sunstone Conference (these are academic conferences that explore LDS theology) in Salt Lake City. He stated that after working in the area of Mesoamerican archaeology for twenty-two years, the scientific evidence simply does not support the existence of the peoples and events chronicled in *The Book of Mormon,* be it in Central America or anywhere else in the Western Hemisphere.

In 1984, I interviewed Dr. Jay Baliff, vice president of academic affairs at BYU, and I asked him if in the Archaeology Department it would be possible to pursue a perfectly legitimate scientific research question: "Is *The Book of Mormon* a true historical account of the cultural history of pre-Columbian American people?" I asked him if the conclusion were that the book was not a historical account, could a Y professor say to his students that he did not believe that gospel?" His answer was no. He said that there are some "given truths" at BYU.

Then I asked Dr. Baliff if a Latter-day Saint professor, regardless of his or her field, was to decide that he or she no longer believed the doctrine of the church, such as *The Book of Mormon,* could he or she continue employment as a professor at the Y? Again his answer was no (Interview with Dr. Jay Baliff at Brigham Young University, December 12, 1984). Yet the Y claims academic freedom.

The Mormon Church claims their members have "free agency," the right to choose in matters of belief. As my friend Wayne Hansen would say, "Free agency, my ass. Free agency, yes; but you damn well better make the right choice." There is no more free choice, no more freedom for most Mormon children or faithful adults to choose in opposition to the church and reach the celestial heaven than there is for a bee not to live in a hive. A true freedom of choice requires freedom of information and choosing without coercion, penalties, or loss of acceptance by peers and family. Wayne used to say with regard to true freedom and the LDS Church, "America giveth and the church taketh away."

Even in the LDS schools of Utah, and some states that border Utah, the LDS Church does not risk losing children to foreign or opposing viewpoints. Arrangements are made whereby high school students may take a very short walk from the school to the LDS seminary building owned by the church. There is the seminary teacher to assure that the Mormon gospel goes out with daily education. Be sure to counter that gentile propaganda about how the Americas were peopled from north Asia, or the improbability of the flood, or the biology of how American Indians got their dark complexion. That is the education from the Saint's seminaries. And to the girls, you have real authority in the church although you cannot hold the priesthood.

In the small Mormon town of Lovell, Wyoming, the high school has a close-by LDS seminary. My PhD student and associate, David Rizor, helped me conduct environmental/conservation education classes for teachers across Wyoming. When we would pass the Lovell High School seminary, he would say, "There's the deprogramming center. What a salesman that Joe Smith was." Is there an American church that spends more energy, time, and more money fixing the thinking of their youth? If the process is successful in youth, the individual's first identity is "Mormon," and they become missionaries and go into the world with the goal of fixing the thinking of the unfamiliar at the doorsteps of the world.

One evening at a friend's home in Monticello, a group of us were discussing the many holes in Joseph Smith's story. Sue Merrill is from a long lineage of Mormons in San Juan County. She said, "How could I give it up (the Joseph Smith story). All of our heritage is in the story." Such is the dilemma, the difficulty, and the sorrow of the society that elevates faith above reason. This is the core of my story. Within the church is security and wellbeing, benefits of community. In a psychological sense, is it worth believing, or at least not denying, the flood story and curses on groups of humans versus rejection or ostracism?

CHAPTER 4

REVELATIONS FOR SURVIVAL

Black 14 Monument at the University of Wyoming

This is the Black 14 Memorial to the fourteen black football players at the University of Wyoming who were dismissed from the University of Wyoming football team by their coach in 1969. The black players refused to play Brigham Young University unless they were allowed to wear black armbands. The LDS Church would not let blacks hold their sacred priesthood until 1978.

There was the usual morning huddle of teachers around the mailboxes that October morning 1969 in the main office at Monticello High School. It appeared from the expressions that the conversation held more excitement than most mornings. As I walked through the open door, I gave the usual greeting to the secretary, Christine Walton, and my colleagues. A quick return of the greeting by the teachers and even quicker return to the conversation indicated to me there was some tattle keeping the teachers from reporting to their classrooms.

I suspected what it was because I had been listening to the sports news in my pickup during the short drive to the school. I stepped close to the group to check my mail. I was right. It was the BYU-Wyoming football predicament. Fourteen black Wyoming football players had been dismissed from the squad because they would not play BYU unless they were allowed to wear black armbands. It was in protest of the racial discrimination policy of the LDS Church. The LDS Church would not let blacks hold their sacred priesthood.

Nine of the players were starters. Lloyd Eaton, the Wyoming coach, dismissed the fourteen players. Though the Wyoming Cowboys crushed the BYU Cougars soundly the next Saturday without the black players (40–7), Wyoming never recovered from the loss of the fourteen athletes. Before they were kicked off the team, Wyoming was off to a 4–0 start and was ranked no. 10 in the country. They ended the season with a 6–4 record and didn't have another winning season until 1976 and didn't play in another bowl game until 1987.

The incident and case received national and international attention and is remembered in the annals of college football as the "The Black 14 Incident." In 1968, after the assassination of Martin Luther King, black members of the University of Texas El Paso (UTEP) track team approached their coach and expressed their desire not to compete against BYU in an upcoming meet. When the coach disregarded the athletes' complaint, the athletes boycotted the meet. In November 1969, Stanford University President Kenneth Pitzer suspended athletic relations with BYU for the church's practice of discriminating against blacks.

The consensus of opinion that morning among the all-Mormon high school teachers was of course in defense of the Wyoming coach. They felt that he had maintained team discipline, and they understood his position that religion had no part in athletic competition. Only five years earlier at BYU, though I was often disgusted with Mormon behaviors and practices, I rooted for their teams. After all, for a short time, I played baseball with them. But suddenly that morning, Rosco Anderson, the art teacher and wrestling coach, put me on the spot. "Duane, you aren't Mormon. What do you think about those blacks at Wyoming refusing to play the Y?"

I thought I would be asked. My answer had already come to me driving to school when I heard the news. I hesitated a moment, as my Mormon friends awaited my opinion. I said, "They're black for the same reason that some black bears are brown. Most black bears are black. Most humans are brown, and some are white. It is well understood in biology." Of course they knew I was the biology teacher. It was time to go to class, and Rosco walked beside me as we went down the hall that divided our rooms. He slapped me on the shoulder and said, "I wish you could understand, Duane. I just wish you could understand."

Let's explore how blacks get cursed through the course of Joseph Smith's revelations as he was giving the Saints their theology. In translating Egyptian, describing the origin of the natives to the Americas, and affixing a date for the lost tribe of Israel's arrival, Smith was out of the realms of theology and metaphysics and into the scientific disciplines of human genetics, archaeology, anthropology, and ethnology. These sciences blossomed and delivered their messages in the twentieth century––messages quite contrary to Smith's. But for bequeathing a millstone around the necks of his descendants through ventures into the domains of science, Smith's gamble with cultural anthropology left little pain relative to his ventures into evolutionary genetics. His disclosure of the reason for coloration of blacks was a cross to be borne by Mormons, which finally became unbearable.

Events leading to Smith's revelation concerning blacks center around his zeal, when he was in his late twenties, to become a master of languages. It was in the early 1830s, with his church founded and headquartered at Kirtland, Ohio, that he began to remedy the shortcomings of his own deficient education and the education of his followers. He had always been intrigued with languages, especially ancient Hebrew, so much so that he hired a young Jewish professor to come to Kirtland and teach him the ancient language.

Ironically, while Smith was ambitiously learning Hebrew, there came to Kirtland a Michael Chandler, who was traveling throughout the country exhibiting four Egyptian mummies and several scrolls that had been discovered by the French explorer Antonio Sebolo. Smith and some of the brethren were so captivated by the artifacts that they purchased the relics at a good price. First, Smith tried interpretation of the scrolls with his newly learned languages. But this not being successful, and under the pressure of the expectations of his following, he turned to the divine power that he had used in translation of the plates into *The Book of Mormon*. He announced to his believing fold that one of the scrolls was the writing of the Old Testament's Abraham and that another scroll contained writings of Joseph of Egypt.

The mummies and the papyri were later lost during the mid-America conflicts with gentiles, but before this misfortune occurred, Joseph Smith copied many of the figures from the scrolls. God reclaimed the golden plates from which *The Book of Mormon* had been translated. But unlike the plates, the copied figures from the Chandler scrolls live on parallel to Joseph Smith's very fanciful translation.

In Kirtland, Ohio, and most regrettably for Smith's reputation as translator, there was no awareness of the nearly simultaneous discovery by the Frenchman, Jean Francois Campollion, of the usefulness of the Rosetta Stone. With the discovery of this ancient Egyptian dictionary, followed by classic and masterful linguistic research to determine its use, the code of the ancient hieroglyphic language was cracked. By the time this knowledge reached the frontier, Joseph had used his divine powers and had already, from his translation of the newly found writings, revised the biblical book of Genesis.

In recent times, the facsimiles of the papyri figures that Joseph translated and published, with elaborate detail, have been pronounced by many Egyptologists to be ordinary funeral documents found within thousands of Egyptian graves. Surprisingly, in 1966, the very papyri from which Joseph Smith copied the ancient Egyptian figures reappeared in the New York Metropolitan Museum[19] (www.en.wikipedia.org/wiki/Book_of_Abraham).

It was from those few figures that Joseph had composed his entire *Book of Abraham*, better known to Mormons as the *Pearl of Great Price*. Along with *The Book of Mormon*, the Bible, and *Doctrine and Covenants* (other revelations by Joseph Smith), it is one of the divine cornerstones of the LDS religion. All Egyptologists, with the exception of the few that were Mormon trained, confirm that the papyri have nothing to say about Abraham or Joseph of Egypt. The Book of Abraham that Smith translated from the papyrus made it divinely right that Mormons not allow blacks to hold the sacred priesthood, and it also gave them "God's" reasons:

> Now this king of Egypt was a descendant from the loins of Ham, and was a partaker of the blood of the Canaanites by birth. From this descent sprang all the Egyptians, and thus the blood of the Canaanites was preserved in the land. The land of Egypt being first discovered by a woman, who was the daughter of Ham, and the daughter Egyptus, which in the Chaldean signifies that which is forbidden. When the woman discovered the land it was under water, who afterward settled her sons in it; and thus, from Ham, sprang that race which preserved the curse in the land.
>
> Now the first government of Egypt was established by Pharoah the eldest son of Egyptus, the daughter of Ham… Pharoah, being a righteous man… seeking earnestly to imitate that order established by the fathers… even in the reign of Adam, and also of Noah, his father, who blessed him with the blessings of wisdom, but cursed him as pertaining to the Priesthood.[20] (*Pearl of Great Price*. Abraham 1:21–26)

Joseph related to his followers that the condition of blacks stemmed from the sin of Ham unto his father, Noah, soon after the great flood.

Neither the Bible nor Joseph Smith elaborated on the sin of Ham, but the punishment for Ham was that his son Canaan would be "servant to servants" (Genesis 9:22). In Civil War time, Southern preachers used this one bit of biblical scripture to justify slavery. Joseph, with the new Egyptian record, elaborated upon the biblical sentence to explain that Pharaoh, the first ruler of Egypt, was the son of Egyptus and that Egyptus was a daughter of the cursed Ham. He told his worshipping followers that all Egyptians had inherited the curse of black skin through Egyptus.

In Joseph's new "restored original Christian church" the curse meant that descendants of Ham could not hold the sacred priesthood, not even deacon, the position of lowest order. Joseph Smith was reflecting an attitude prevalent at the time, which would have disappeared, officially at least, with nearly all institutions. For Mormons, however, through the young prophet's translation, the word became divine guidance and scripture.

From 1835 until 1978, the monstrous precept hung on the necks of Mormons to cause them ridicule and shame. Finally, the pain became too much. For modern Mormons residing in an America striving to fulfill the founding fathers' doctrine it came to an end. It was ended as nearly as it could be without rebuking the entire concept of revelation. By revelation to the late president of the church and modern-day prophet, Spencer Kimball, God gave blacks the privilege of the priesthood.

Here is what John Farrell, *The Denver Post* author who wrote a series about Mormons in the 1980s, said concerning the day President and Prophet Spencer Kimball announced the revelation:

June 9, 1978, was the day grown men cried in Salt Lake
City. Some heard the news on the radio, pulled cars to
the side of the road and wept with gratitude. Others
wiped tears from their cheeks as they gathered in the
grandeur of Temple Square. The city's phone system
strained as Mormons from all over the world tried to
call relatives to ask if it was true. Years later, just as some
remember Pearl Harbor or the November day in Dallas,
Saints can tell you precisely where they were and what
they were doing when the Prophet Spencer Kimball
announced that the Mormon priesthood had finally
been opened to the Blacks.[21] (*The Denver Post [Empire
Magazine]*, p. 17, Nov. 28, 1982)

It wasn't only the civil rights marches around the temple, and universities
refusing to schedule BYU. In Brazil, the LDS Church built a temple,
and it was about to be dedicated. But who were the blacks? In Brazil,
there are so many persons who are mulattos, persons of mixed Caucasian
and black ancestry. The following interview was conducted on August
16, 1978, at the church's office building. The interviewer was Wesley
Walters, and the person interviewed was Mormon Apostle LeGrand
Richards. This excerpt was taken from the LDS Church website (www.
ldsmormon.com/legrand_richards.shtml Walters–Richards interview).

Walters: On this revelation, of the priesthood to the
Negro, I've heard all kinds of stories: I've heard that
Joseph Smith appeared; and then I heard another story
that Spencer Kimball had had a concern about this for
some time, and simply shared it with the apostles, and
they decided that this was the right time to move in that
direction. Are any of those stories true, or are they all?

Richards: Well, the last one is pretty true, and I might
tell you what provoked it in a way. Down in Brazil,

there is so much Negro blood in the population there that it's hard to get leaders that don't have Negro blood in them. We just built a temple down there. It's going to be dedicated in October.

All those people with Negro blood in them have been raising the money to build that temple. If we don't change, then they can't even use it. Well, Brother Kimball worried about it, and he prayed a lot about it.[22] (Interview with Apostle LeGrand Richards by Wesley P. Walters and Chris Vlachos, August 16, 1978, church office building, [recorded on cassette])

By the mid-1970s the church officials as well as the membership had simply endured enough. The discriminatory policy toward blacks had the potential to destroy the church. The issue almost daily caused adverse publicity. There were mock ordinations of blacks into the priesthood even outside the gates of Salt Lake Temple. But suddenly it was over. Even more quickly than Smith's saga had become scripture, the racist policy was swept out with Kimball's revelation. Not once during the twentieth century had Mormon faith in their prophet been demonstrated such as it was with the lifting of the curse concerning the priesthood. As Farrell describes it, "Four million Mormons (This was in 1982, now there are nearly fourteen million) woke up that morning believing that Blacks were cursed, but went to bed that night believing with an open heart, willing to accept those of African descent as priests"[23] (*The Denver Post [Empire Magazine]*, p. 20, Nov. 28, 1982). The 2012 U.S. presidential race is upon us and Mitt Romney is the Republican candidate. He is a lifelong Mormon. A comment about the revelation concerning blacks and the priesthood has gone viral on the worldwide web. Above Romney holding a stern face it says "I believe." Below his picture is, "In 1978 God changed his mind about blacks."

In the 1800s, racial inferiority was believed widely and reinforced by some scientists. Though pockets of racism remain, for humankind, the nineteenth and twentieth centuries were our most glorious centuries. Belief that some races were inferior wasn't only out of academia, but in 1964, denouncement of "superior" and "inferior" races went into the United Nations Educational, Scientific and Cultural Organization (UNESCO) charter. By 1978, in U.S. politics, a sure defeat for nearly all politicians was to be linked with racism, even in our South. The Mormon Church had only one course to take for survival. Revelation or reality?

So why do LDS believe this change to their theology came by revelation? Because scriptures had to be changed. Revelations are necessary to change the Saint's scriptures. But why didn't God or the prophet accept the real challenge? The real curse, as it must be viewed by Mormons, is the black skin, the flatter nose, larger lips, more sweat glands in the skin, and greater resistance to skin cancer?

And let's add athleticism. Follow the National Basketball Association teams or the running backs in the National Football Association teams. Yesterday, I watched on TV the finals in the National College Athletic Association track and field meet in Des Moines, Iowa. All of the finalists in the men and women's one-hundred-meter and two-hundred-meter races were black. These are all part of the package in being black. These traits were selected, most for survival, through the course of human evolution in the African environment, as were blue eyes and fair skin selected in the northern climates. Except within societies that have been authoritatively poisoned against the ideas of organic evolution— which explains variation in skin color and a myriad of other human variations—the natural selection principles today are in the Copernican realm of science.

The real challenge for the Mormon prophet in June of 1978 would have been to remove the black traits, as Mormons must view the curse of blacks "revealed" by their founding prophet. It is his revelation just as sure as Joseph told his fold how the Americans Indians got here, or that he was their prophet. It was so simple for the modern-day prophet Spencer Kimball to give Africans their priesthood in 1978.

For us 3 percent who entered BYU as nonmembers, the first religion class was generally "religion for non-LDS." Some students, with much more awareness of Mormon theology and history than I, would have questions that were probably meant to put the instructor on the defensive. I remember the question posed to the instructor about the Saints practicing polygamy. Throughout America at the turn of the nineteenth century it was, and for many gentiles, still is, the identifying feature of the faith, even through it has been more than one hundred years since the Utah church approved it. "Polygamy came from God," was the answer. "Then why did it end," is the follow up question. Again, the LDS answer goes to God. "He took it away."

In high school history classes, most students come away with three references to Mormons. First is their persecution in the Midwest that caused them to follow in the way of Moses and seek the wilderness, which was for them the Great Basin of Utah. Second, they practiced polygamy, and this put them in big trouble with American society, and third, they have a prophet who receives revelations from God, and it is through the revelations the Saints do right. And I need to add, change their practices of the first Christian church of the Old Testament when the revealed road becomes impassable.

The practice of polygamy by Latter-day Saints through the second half of the nineteenth century became the great isolating mechanism and added to the "them" vs. "us" dichotomy. And by the time of the Civil War, polygamy and slavery were considered the twin barbarisms of American society. However, for the Saints, polygamy was divine reverence. The defense of its practice was a defense of God's way, and the opponents were, if not of the devil, at least ignorant of the rules of the Lord's righteous kingdom.

In 1882, the mood of America opposed polygamy to the extent that Congress passed the Edmunds Act. It disqualified George Q. Cannon from becoming the Utah Territorial Representative by declaring polygamy a felony. It also disenfranchised polygamists, nullified their eligibility for office and jury duty, and placed territorial elections under the control of a presidential commission. The commission had the authority and responsibility to disqualify any candidate for election who was a polygamist.

The church and its membership openly defied the Edmunds Act. Prominent Mormon leaders who were polygamists went underground to avoid arrest by the federal authorities sent to Utah to enforce the law. The president of the church at the time, John Taylor, died while hiding from the law. He had been in the Carthage jail in Missouri with Joseph Smith and was wounded when their prophet was murdered by the mob. That he should die while avoiding what the Saints considered religious persecution made him a "double martyr" and further hardened the sentiments of the Saints toward the outside world. But no amount of rationalizing the need or benefit of polygamy by the Saints could offset the bitter pain caused by those proactive against it. It was given scandalous hype by the press, and social muckrakers would return from Utah to their soapboxes in the East to stir up the remnants of Puritanism that remained in the hearts of many Americans.

This publicity only further entrenched the practice of polygamy in Mormondom, where left alone, it may have died a sooner death. To keep it alive required continuous admonitions from the prophet and his priests, the same kind of doublethink that is used today to describe Mormon free agency or women's freedom and authority in the church. That polygamy was a prevalent problem to the development of the church is evidenced by the frequency with which sermons centered on plurality of wives. When asked by Horace Greeley in 1859, Brigham Young said that he had fifteen wives; however, the reported number goes as high as fifty-six. One Sunday, September 21, 1856, Brigham Young threatened to free all of his whining wives as well as the others of the community[24] (*Journal of Discourses*, pp. 55–57, vol. 4).

> Now for my proposition; it is more particularly for my sisters, as it is frequently happening that women say they are unhappy. Men will say, "My wife, though a most excellent woman, has not seen a happy day since I took my second wife," "No, not a happy day for a year, says one; and another has not seen a happy day for five years. It is said that women are tied down and abused: that they are misused and have not the liberty they ought to have; that many of them are wading through a perfect flood of tears…" I wish my own women to understand that what I am going to say is for them as well as others, and I want those who are here to tell their sisters, yes, all the women of this community, and then write it back to

the States, and do as you please with it. I am going to give you from this time to the 6th day of October next, for reflection, that you may determine whether you wish to stay with your husbands or not, and then I am going to set every woman at liberty and say to them, Now go your way, my women with the rest, go your way. And my wives have got to do one of two things; either round up their shoulders to endure the afflictions of this world, and live their religion, or they may leave, for I will not have them about me. I will go into heaven alone, rather than have scratching and fighting around me. I will set all at liberty. "What, first wife too?" Yes, I will liberate you all…

For five years, the federal authorities tried to enforce the Edmunds Act without success: the laws of God proved to be of higher priority than those of the U.S. Congress. In 1887, Congress passed the Edmunds-Tucker Act to notify Mormons of the seriousness of the matter. This law restricted the provisions of the previous act and took away all property of the Latter-day Saint Church valued at more than $50,000. This property was to be sold, and the funds used to finance the schools of the territory. President/Prophet Wilford Woodruff explained to the fold the abandonment of polygamy. At the Cache Stake Conference, Logan, Utah, Sunday, November 1, 1891, as reported in *Deseret Weekly*, November 14, 1891, he said,

The Lord showed me by vision and revelation exactly what would take place if we did not stop this practice. If we had not stopped it, you would have had no use for… any of the men in this temple at Logan; for all ordinances would be stopped throughout the land of Zion. Confusion would reign throughout Israel, and many men would be made prisoners. This trouble would have come upon the whole Church, and we should have been compelled to stop the practice. Now, the question is, whether it should be stopped in this manner, or in the way the Lord has manifested to us, and leave our Prophets and Apostles and fathers free men, and the temples in the hands of the people, so that the dead may be redeemed. A large number has already been delivered from the prison house in the spirit world by this people, and shall the work go on or stop? This is the question I lay before the Latter-day Saints. You have to judge for yourselves. I want you to answer it for yourselves. I shall not answer it; but I say to you that that is exactly the condition we as a people would have been in had we not taken the course we have.

I saw exactly what would come to pass if there was not something done. I have had this spirit upon me for a long time. But I want to say this: I should have let all the temples go out of our hands; I should have gone to prison myself, and let every other man go there, had not the God of heaven commanded me to do what I did do; and when the hour came that I was commanded to do that, it was all clear to me. I went before the Lord, and I wrote what the Lord told me to write....

I leave this with you, for you to contemplate and consider. The Lord is at work with us.[25] (www.lds.org/scriptures/dc-testament/od/1?lang=eng [website of the LDS Church])

The revelation, known today as the Woodruff Manifesto, came in 1890, but it was hard to enforce, even with God's revelation, and the U.S. government was not satisfied with polygamy ending until January 4, 1896, when the state joined the nation. Today polygamy is gone from the mainstream of Mormon culture, and any practitioners in the Utah church are excommunicated. After nearly a half century of open practice, it was discontinued for the preservation of the Church and the hope of the Mormon people to be accepted into the United States.

The faithful LDS will say that God's revelations prove how flexible and changeable God's advice can be. After all, can't God change his mind? Other religions have tenets that remain unchanged, and they cause the religion struggles in modern times.

The end of the nineteenth century was a time of turbulent adjustment in Utah. As in the Midwest fifty years earlier, gentiles surrounded the planned Kingdom of God which had originally been the Territory of Deseret (Deseret is a *Book of Mormon* term meaning "honey bee"). It included Utah and Nevada, large portions of California and Arizona, and parts of Colorado, New Mexico, Wyoming, Idaho, and Oregon. The hope for a religious kingdom for the Saints had long since vanished, and roads and railroad tracks wound through what had been a purely Mormon province. Surrounding Utah, the other territories that had been carved from the vast Territory of Deseret were one by one meeting the requirements and joining the Union. But in Utah, the issue of polygamy and a church-dominated political system frightened the U.S. Congress. But in truth, America was and may still be biased against the Mormon brand of Christianity. The American people have given major denominations of Christianity the advantage in elections, though the U.S. and state constitutions separate religion from government. How many openly atheists and agnostics serve in those governments?

For nearly fifty years, the official government of Utah had been appointed in Washington, which had long been a thorn in the backside of the Saints. Their true government, the one respected and obeyed, was the prophet and his priests. But by the turn of the century, the

Kingdom of God, the gathering of Zion, the perfect agrarian communal society, the Second Coming of Christ to usher in the millennium, so many of the hopes that had silently filled the mountain valleys with Mormon pilgrims, were disappearing like the mirages in the western Utah desert.

Because the Saints were firm in their belief that it was their constitutionally protected religious right to practice polygamy, when the prophet finally surrendered this practice, its end was slowly accepted. Even the Saints turned monogamous would not be put asunder by the U.S. government, a government of man. But the command from God, through the prophet Wilford Woodruff, finally ended plural marriage.

Most revelations since Joseph Smith and Brigham Young have come in order to survive the revelations of the first two prophets. Smith's revelations that caused radical and socially intolerant practices required revelations by his successors.

Not all significant changes in the cornerstone Mormon theology documents have required revelations. There was the "white and delightsome" change in 1981. It paralleled changing social times though it has proved embarrassing since *The Book of Mormon* was said by Joseph Smith to be "the most correct of any book on earth, and the keystone of our religion." However, in the aftermath of the riotous civil rights days, when skin color was the focus of marches and demonstrations, authorities of the church believed wording in a particular sentence of their gospel was a red flag.

A change in a new edition of *The Book of Mormon* was printed without announcement. But it was discovered by Mormon watchers and printed in the *Los Angeles Times*, October 1, 1981.[26] The change alters a prophecy that American Indians who join the Church of Jesus Christ of Latter-day Saints will become "white and delightsome." The new edition of the book, and all those since, says American Indian converts will become a "pure and delightsome people." After such changes, is the book still the word of God? The rub for Latter-day Saints is that in order to take an active step toward changing old ideas and to have a new beginning in their relationship with the dark peoples of the world, God's word in their scriptures must be changed, overlooked, or ignored. This is not impossible—the Saints have shown this in the past—but for some, it shakes faith and obedience, the prime requisites of being Mormon. Some will not accept the new revelations and will carry their original scriptures, as they were, to the grave. Witness the offshoots from the Utah church practicing polygamy. They continually make the public media.

CHAPTER 5

WHERE HAVE ALL THE FLOWERS GONE?

With natural reproduction from within, Utah has filled the valleys.

I'll read it but it won't change my mind.

—A southern Utah Mormon mother
when asked to read *The Population Bomb*

Man masters nature not by force but by understanding.
This is why science has succeeded where magic failed:
because it has looked for no spell to cast over nature.

—Jacob Bronowski

"Duane, there are some mothers in the hall looking at the posters." I could sense the anxiety of Darlene Harley, my loyal and respectful secretary, as she spoke to me from the doorway to my office. The topic of the posters, overpopulation, had caused her nervousness too. She was a Mormon. I had hung the posters in the hallway and on a main bulletin board at the San Juan Junior High School in Blanding, Utah. The posters informed about the challenging and many-faceted problems stemming from overpopulation. The occasion was the third celebration of Earth Day, April 1973. They were purchased from the Welsh Publishing Group, a reputable supplier of school supplies. There were scenes of crowded beaches and parks, U.S. surplus milk being destroyed in Wisconsin, several more posters illustrating the problems of failed distribution systems, the slums of Mexico City, and too many mouths to feed.

When I assumed the principalship at the San Juan Junior High School, I was just completing a doctorate in Biology and Curriculum and my thesis concerned planning curricula for environmental education. I knew the Mormons and their mores and especially their sacred beliefs about getting the many spirit children onto earth to be tested in preparation for eternal life, be it the highest celestial kingdom or a lesser life in the hereafter. I wanted to be careful, even subtle. But the four LDS mothers in the hall were a sure sign that I had not been careful or subtle enough.

From my office I walked into the hall and greeted the ladies. I was friendly and courteous as I escorted them into my office and seated them to talk. As I began to discuss the topics of the posters, it was obvious the women had only taken a superficial look at the issues and problems the posters illustrated. Any viewing of the posters at all was not necessary. It was the topic. The Saints are sensitive to criticism about having too many children. The ladies had not met each other in front of the posters at a designated time to learn about population problems. I began my defense of the posters.

I told the four mothers of junior high students the posters were for Earth Day and that the World Health Organization ranked population control—it was in 1973—as the greatest challenge in human history. From the life science text in use at the school, I showed them that the topic was an integral component of the environmental education chapter and not a personal add-on by the principal. I remember turning in the text to the exponential graph that showed the J curve growth in human population. They seemed to be listening. Perhaps I was making four unexpected converts to this important concept in environmental ethics, and conservation of natural resources. After all, it was the environmental decade, and ecology was as American as apple pie.

One of my last classes in graduate school was titled "Man and the Environment," and Paul and Anne Erlich's bestseller, *The Population Bomb,* had been assigned reading. I reached for a copy of the book on a shelf near my desk. Generously, I suggested to Mrs.White, spokeslady for the mothers, that she might like to read the book. "I'll read it, but it won't change my mind," she declared. I welcomed the ladies back to the school and followed them to the door. Before returning to the office, I reread the posters. I was only beginning to learn about the competition of science understanding with "heart truths."

In the middle of that afternoon, Mary Nelson, vice president of the San Juan County School Board, arrived at my office, the only time I remember her visiting the school. She strode right into my office, ignoring my secretary. "I'm here as a mother," she announced. Her son was in the eighth grade. "It's the posters," she continued. "They have to come down. You just don't understand the church and this community." I let her talk and didn't try to counter her argument, hoping her already-ignited fuse would burn out before I would try to persuade her that the posters had a place in the school. But she was not there only as a parent. The mothers wanted her to defend the community.

She saw that I was not easily dissuaded and that I understood the Mormon position in advance of hanging the posters. I reminded her that the Indian children held a slight majority in our student population, and they were not Mormon. They and the Mormon children had a right to know about the problems of the world. I recall telling Mrs. Nelson that I had taught on the Navajo reservation, and for two weekends, I traveled to the homes of the people and took the school population count. That is a count of all children in the homes, necessary for school planning. Utah state law requires the school census.

My count told the school district and the state that in the Aneth region of the Navajo reservation, the average number of children in each home was five, as many or more children as in the Mormon homes. I explained that our teachers had an obligation to teach about ramifications of overpopulation and organic evolution. Though they may be contrary to some parents' religious beliefs, they were grounded in much scientific evidence. "Do you believe in evolution too?" she demanded. I said, "I'm qualified to be your school principal, Mrs. Nelson, but I am also a biologist and a biology educator. Organic evolution is the framework of our understanding of modern biology."

"I want those posters down," she warned and left.

The next day Dr. Kendal Popham, the assistant superintendent and curriculum director for San Juan School District, and a Mormon, was an early morning inspector of the posters. "Duane," he said, "this district has enough problems without the posters." On the minds of the district administrators was a lawsuit about to be filed by the Navajo Tribe demanding the construction of high schools on the reservation. "You better take them down." I did. To hell with science. "Heart truths" had won for Blanding. Utah was still a theocracy as in the nineteenth century.

I had tested the bond. But more importantly, what I had learned in biology, human ecology, and natural resources conservation would not be shared openly with the Blanding students, or the Navajo students. Hindsight is twenty-twenty. I should have left the posters up and tested in court the message they told—for other teachers to know the power of Amendment Number One. More than thirty years have passed since the posters came down at the junior high school. During those years, Utah has doubled its population with natural internal reproduction, just as the demographers of 1980 said it would.

There is another reflection on the posters incident. The fact that I would or could put the posters on the walls for the students to learn of a real problem not addressed in Mormondom is a study in itself. Would an LDS principal who was a biologist have exercised the authority of his or her position to go counter to the culture? What would have been the Mormon's psychological and social consequences with unraveling this intimate and supportive network? There is great value in freedom of thought and the search for solutions to human problems. However, parents trust the school leader to give the children life lessons that are not counter to their religious guidance. A Mormon principal's conundrum would have been that of a BYU biology professor, except the parents were next door.

I remember well the fall in 1983, when I returned to the Utah Valley to begin the project that finally is this book. It was the year of my sabbatical from the University of Wyoming, the year I surveyed student opinion on religious/science beliefs. I rented an apartment in a home near the University of Utah campus. In September and in the great Wasatch Range, to the east of Salt Lake, the color begins to stream down the western slopes. First high at the top of the peaks, where there was already a dusting of snow, the aspen were in patches of yellow; and in the canyons, the maple dotted the hillsides with shades of orange. On the valley floor in Salt Lake, a mile and a half down from the snow line, the exotic trees that line the streets remained luxuriantly green, unaware of the chill that nightly crept down the mountains. The descending cold would soon leave the stately Wasatch Range a patchwork of splendor, and Utah would be at its prime.

The physical beauty of Utah is unmatched. The upwarp of the earth's crust in combination with the sculpturing by weathering and erosion has made the state the international monument to the geological history and age of the earth. Tourists swarm the Beehive State throughout the seasons in awe of naturally carved stone monuments that reveal the time before man. Utah has more national parks and monuments than any other state (save Alaska and California). Each one speaks of eras past: when Utah was a great white-sand desert, a huge inland sea, miles of red mudflats at an ocean's edge, great lakes and rivers full of the thaw from the Ice Age, and the earth's crust cracking to form the Wasatch

Range. From the alpine meadows in the Uinta Mountains to the red-rock shores of Lake Powell lies a region of unparalleled geological and ecological diversity.

For more than a century and a half on this land, a religious culture has been scurrying about, building temples, baptizing the dead, and doing the rituals they see as necessary in readying themselves for judgment day. Most Saints are oblivious to the meaning of the earth record beneath their feet and geology's relationship to human time and culture. Legend has it that Ebenezer Bryce, the Mormon discoverer of Bryce Canyon, said as he looked across that great chasm dug by nature into sediments of environments past, "That's a hell-of-a-place to lose a cow." Give the old fellow credit; he became an amateur geologist. Whether or not Bryce made that remark, it does humorously point out the disjuncture for many Mormons with natural science and the natural beauty that is our earth. After all, to them this life is the testing field for our status in the eternal life.

The Latter-day Saints immigrated to the Territory of Deseret beginning in 1847 to build Zion. Some called it the Kingdom of God. The kingdom was to be built before the second coming of Christ. Utah is the geological Mecca for exposure of earth's history and geological processes. The state is the antithesis of Joseph Smith's reincarnated Old Testament time frame of earth and human history. Of course, Brigham Young and his followers who were farmers, not geologists, did not know the meaning of the rocks, especially as we do today.

In place of stratigraphy, they had the Bible and their prophet's revealed scriptures. They built their society around what they were told by their religious leaders. Today, because science cannot be ignored at any accredited university, even at Brigham Young University, one might hear a geology professor at the Y's Eyring Science Center telling students about the 4.6-billion-year-old earth's geological and evolutionary events. This while across the hall, a Mormon theology professor rationalizes the creation of earth in six days and may ask students to pray for an affirmation of the validity of the church's gospel truths.

The people of developed nations such as the United States look with alarm at most Third World countries' growth rates. Dr. Paul Erlich, the famous population ecologist at Stanford University and author of *The Population Bomb*, has a useful analogy. He says that for countries with stable populations and growth rates to look without alarm at Third World nations with populations growing beyond their resources is like one man in a canoe telling the man in the other end of the canoe that his end of the canoe is sinking.

People without resources, especially food, cannot be ignored. Our Judeo Christian conscience will not allow it. Or for that matter, some of us are not content to let very wealthy nations use a completely disproportionate share of the resources. The yearly consumption of energy in kilograms of oil equivalent units per capita in the United States is 7,886 kg compared to 532 kg for Tanzania[27] (www.earthtrends.wri.org/text/energy-resources/variable-351.html). Two years ago, I returned from Tanzania and Kenya. My most memorable recollection is not the elephants and wildlife of Serengeti or climbing Kilimanjaro, which are unforgettable, but how much Americans use and how little Tanzanians use.

Some of the Erlich's predictions have not come about, largely because of our continuing betterment of agricultural production. And reproduction rates world over have gone down since 1968 when the book was published. The world growth rate peaked at 2.2 percent in 1963 and declined to 1.1 percent by 2009. The Erlich's best-selling book deserves some of the credit. It was an alert for the world. Many countries have reached zero population growth, and the doubling times of some that were less than thirty years in 1968 have been vastly lengthened. But some food sources are nearing exhaustion. The ocean's fisheries are the whole world's example. Yearly, they produce less of favored species than the previous year, and the price continues to climb.

The population of Utah in 1980 was 1,461,000, and the annual increase for that year was 2.6 percent. At that rate of increase, the doubling time would be 33.1 years. The results from the 2010 Census are in and Utah is ahead of the mark. With two years to double, the 2010 population is 2,784,000. The doubling time in 2010 is predicted to be 33 years, which means in 2044, the population of Zion will be 5,569,000. The U.S. population stands at 308,745,500. That represents 27.3 million more people than in 2000, or 9.7 percent increase in the U.S. population. A large portion of this increase is through immigration, and much of the immigration has been illegal.

The increase in Utah during the same time period was 20 percent. The number of people added to the U.S. population between 2000 and 2010 was lower than it was during the 1990s. Utah's birth rate in 2010 was 21.7 per thousand compared with the national average of 13.9 per thousand. According to the Population Reference Bureau, the 21.7 births per thousand in Utah is higher than Mexico (19/1,000), Peru, Ecuador, Venezuela (21/1,000), and Azerbaijan in Western Asia (17/1,000). In 2006, 83.2 of every one thousand women in Utah gave birth, and the national average was 54.9. The New Hampshire rate for 2006 was half that of Utah at 42 per thousand.

According to the U.S. Census Bureau, Utah has the youngest population. In Utah, 31.2 percent are under eighteen years of age. For 2011, Utah's Education Association reports more than eleven thousand new registered students. Family size is starving students of educational opportunities. Utah is at the bottom of the list in the states for amount spent per student. According to the U.S. Census Bureau, Utah spends an average of $5,683 per year educating each student. The biggest spender, New York, spends three times as much, $15, 981, and the neighboring state of Wyoming spends $13, 217 per child. Like Wyoming, Utah is rich in natural resources, especially minerals.

A continual war is waged in the Beehive State between parents with small families, mostly gentiles, and large families. Utah is about 40 percent non-Mormon. These families reside mainly in the Salt Lake area. Logically, they ask why they must pay school taxes for two children that equal taxes paid by a family with five or more children. Fair it isn't, but in the school boards and the state legislature, the Mormon fathers with large families dominate. About 80 percent of Utah's Legislature are members of the Church of Jesus Christ of Latter-day Saints[28] ("The Church's Growth, Structure and Reach," *The Mormons*. PBS.org. April 2007).

And they have a religious mission that is eternal. The growth rate of Utah has for decades strained the fabric of the society. But in the last decade, it isn't just Utah natural reproduction that strains the fabric. Hispanics accounted for 78 percent of the growth in Utah over the last decade and now make up 13 percent of the Utah population. The LDS Church has a significant presence in Mexico and has come out in favor of a very liberal "love thy neighbor" state immigration policy. There are more Mormon missionaries in Latin America than any other region of the world. For the Saints, Mexicans and other Latinos are Lamanites, descendants of the cursed Laman. It is ironic, but testimony to biological ignorance about their origin, the theology of the LDS, or both, that Latin Americans represent such a growing percentage of the Mormon population.

Saints will tell you they believe that each family should have as many children for whom the parents can adequately provide. Following their theology, Saints believe in "eternal progression." In another existence, there are spirit children that must come to the earth. Earth life is a testing time in the progression. On earth, each person has the opportunity to prepare for differing degrees of reward in heaven. In the celestial afterlife, the heaven with the most rewards, some will become gods, like the god the Saints worship. They believe spirit children born into a large Mormon family are much favored. There will be greater glory in heaven for parents who haven't limited their family size.

I talked with the late Dr. Sterling McMurrin about LDS family size among other topics. Dr. McMurrin was an honored professor of philosophy at the University of Utah and was President John F. Kennedy's Secretary of Education before there was a Department of Education. He was the intellectual dean of Mormonism. He didn't believe any Mormon scriptures were divine. I asked him if there were any theological writings that direct Mormons to have big families. He said he knew of none. "Mormons just like big families," he said. It is more complex. Compelling for having many children, as anthropologists and psychologists will acknowledge, is the enormous social pressure brought on by membership in the Mormon group. There is great social satisfaction in being as spiritual as your neighbor. The large family earns one acceptance in the group.

Human numbers and their sustainability with natural resources is a neglected topic in the school curriculum and not just in Utah. Mormons help us focus on the issue, but they are not unique—just a very vivid example. Mormons marry young. They would do well to know the histories of societies that exhaust their natural resources.

Jared Diamond's best selling book, *Collapse,* is about histories of cultures that expand and consume beyond their natural resources base. Archeological records tell demographers that there were 200–300 million humans on the earth in AD 1. By 1650, there were 500 million, and as late as 1850, there were one billion of us. Today, there are 7,064,804,100 of our species. That was our number at 8:05 AM, September 7, 2012. With technology the information age gives us, counting our numbers has become a precise science.

I do not type fast, but since I wrote down 7,064,804,100, four hundred more were born. This year as of September 7th, 90,795,084 babies have been born and 38,777,875 deaths have occurred. That is right. There have been about 52 million more births than deaths that have occurred in the first eight months and seven days off 2012.[29] (www. worldometers.info). The generation that was born in the 1930s—that includes myself—will be the only generation in world history to ever see world population double, and even triple, in their lifetime. How did this happen? Why did this happen? There is basic biology and simple mathematics involved. The mathematics was discovered in the late eighteenth century by Thomas Malthus (1766–1834), a British reverend and intellectual. Charles Darwin and Alfred Wallace used the work of Malthus to explain natural selection, the mechanism of organic evolution.

Earlier, I spoke of the class "Man and the Environment" I took in the last semester of the doctorate courses at Ball State University. My advisor, Dr. Clyde Hibbs, taught the class. The first day of class, he put this equation on the board.

$$\frac{\text{a country's resources}}{\text{number of people}} \times \text{technology factor} = \text{standard of living}$$

Immediately, a student asked, "How about Japan and the Netherlands? They don't have hardly any resources and they live very well." Dr. Hibbs said that was always the first question when he put the equation on the board. He explained that Japan and the Netherlands have been importing resources for centuries, and their technology factors are the highest in the world. He said it takes about one acre of arable land to grow each person's food. Then he plugged numbers into the equation to test it with math.

But does the equation work today with international trade? In the United States, we eat strawberries from South America, and cars and computers are made with parts manufactured all over the world. Yes, it remains true today. We only need the adage that I saw as a bumper sticker, "God made earth and it has been the same size ever since." At this time, the oceans are overfished and nearly all of earth's arable land is under cultivation. The rainforests are coming down to raise crops and cattle. For the last fifty years, world population multiplied more rapidly than ever before. But, with a sigh of relief, growth in human numbers was more rapid in the last century than it is projected for the twenty-first century. In 1950, the world had 2.5 billion people; and in 2005, the world had 6.5 billion people. By 2050, this number could rise to more than 9 billion[30] (www.prb.org/.../HumanPopulation/PopulationGrowth. aspx - Cached - Similar Population Reference Bureau – Google).

The earth is one pie and to divide it among us all with growing numbers, the slices must be smaller. The most important factor in reducing the rate of population growth has been the education of women.

Every species has what biologists call its biotic potential. The biotic potential is the number of individuals the species would produce if all survived. Following is a passage from the most-used biology book in America in 1973, *Modern Biology*, by James H. Otto and Albert Towle, published by Holt, Rinehart, and Winston.[31] It was the most-used text the year the population posters went up.

> At a single spawning, an oyster may shed 114,000,000 eggs. If all these eggs survived, the ocean would be literally filled with oysters. Within five generations, there would be more oysters than the estimated number of electrons in the visible universe! There is, however, no such actual increase.

> The elephant is considered to have a slow rate of reproduction. An average elephant lives to be 100 years old, breeds over a span of 30 to 90 years, and bears about 6 young. Yet if all the young from one pair of elephants survived, in 750 years the descendants would number 19,000,000.

From a mating pair, how many organisms must continuously survive and reproduce in order for the species to continue? Only two. Then why are so many offspring produced? It is a survival mechanism. Most offspring do not reach reproductive age. They die before reproducing.

In the last two centuries, a steadily increasing percentage of human offspring survive to reproduce.

For thousands of years, the same laws of survival as for other species governed the human species, and the number of humans remained rather constant. Why did the number of humans begin to increase? The elementary reason is that fewer died. For most of our species' existence, we were prey to war—which hasn't changed—breach births, and thousands of other forms of fatality. But with the coming of agriculture, about seven thousand years ago, no longer did the species have to be hunters and gatherers and pack their newborn children, a limiting factor in how many children a woman can bear. Without agriculture, the fertility rate was low. But with the development of agriculture, more children were born, and there was more food to feed them. With more food came populations with more dense numbers, and they were more subject to disease. The Black Plague in Europe (1348–1350) took about one-fourth of the population.

In the secondary curriculum manual of an environmental education program I developed at the University of Wyoming is an activity called "Growthville, USA"[32] ("Growthville, USA," *Wild Wonderful Wyoming* [Secondary Activities Manual], Duane Keown, University of Wyoming, 1998). Students do the math and discover the numbers of community members resulting from families with four children, compared with families with two children. They work like demographers with a set of assumptions and carry out the math. Below is the student activity page of the exercise. Note the beginning population of Growthville in 1998 was 2,000.

Growthville, USA
Population 2,000 in 1998

Two Possible Growth Scenarios
(1) A Four Children Family and
(2) A Two Children Family

Assumptions about Growthville and the growth prediction process.

1. Males and females are equal in number, 1,000 males and 1,000 females.

2. The childbearing age of women is 18 through 40, or 22 years. There are few exceptions.

3. Average life expectancy for the people of Growthville is the same in 1998 as it was for the rest of Wyoming, 79 years for females, and 73 years for men. The average life expectancy for both genders was 75.5 years (use 76 years).

4. Women bearing children would represent **22/79 of the female population in 1998.** Or shown graphically below:

$$*\_\_\_\_\_22/79\_\_\_\_\_*$$

0,1,2,3,4,5,6...........18----------------40, 41, 42, ...76, 77, 78,79

Growthville women of childbearing age in 1998 equals 22/79 × 1000, or 278 females.

5. People in Growthville who are 18 years of age in 1998 were born in 1980. Their average life expectancy in 1998

is 76 years. In 76 years, the population in 1998 will all be gone from the population, with a few exceptions. In order to calculate the deaths in the population, every 76 years deduct the population number 76 years before. If the population in the year 1998 was 2,000, all of those persons will have expired by AD 2,074.

Every 22 years, the proportion of the female population that is between 18 and 40 years of age produces four children in the "four children" section of the activity, and two children in the "two children" section of the activity.

The population of Growthville would be 14,797 in AD 2123 if the number of children in the families averaged four. Of course, the population remains two thousand if the children number two. The scenario above is oversimplified, but the principles and the math go on over time around the earth. The math is simple. The consequences of too many people and too few resources should not escape the prophet of the LDS Church. Nor should it escape the pope or the grand ayatollah of the Muslim religion. A simple statement by the Mormon prophet or the leaders of the burgeoning religious groups would turn our numbers around before we reach the cliff.

Like the men in the canoe, LDS growth rate affects us all, especially we who share the Rocky Mountains. Depending on the measurement of the loss of environmental quality, many would say the cliff was reached years ago. Some countries have stable populations; some have doubling times of less than that of a generation and some, like Italy in the shadow of the Vatican, have negative population growth. The literacy rate for women in Italy is 98.5 percent. Some countries in South America under great influence of the Catholic Church, but with low levels of education for women, have the population doubling times of Utah. Utah, in just over a generation, your space per person will be halved. There may be double the number of cars on the highways, double the number of people in the parks, and double the consumption of food and less farm land to produce the food. Nearly all of Utah Valley has gone under pavement for stores, homes, motels, churches and schools—the stuff to sustain the numbers. Most of Utah's food is now imported.

The problems of overpopulating Utah were recognized as early as 1885. By the 1890s, nearly all of Utah's good arable farmland had been taken, and the vocation of farming was everywhere present. R. A. Hamond, in the *Deseret News* (April 29, 1885), the Salt Lake Mormon newspaper, wrote,

> I find the settlements crowded to their capacity, land and water all appropriated, and our young people as they marry often have no place to settle near home… the resources of the people are all about exhausted unless they go into manufacturing.[33]

If Hamond could see it now: at the present growth rate of Utah, in 156 years, just from Utah, the Latter-day Saint population's natural reproduction will cause a doubling of the U.S. population were the rest of the U.S. population to remain the same as in 2011. The Saints may look at this projection and rejoice to think that finally their church will have great influence upon the life of this nation and the world. They may see it, finally, as the emergence of the Kingdom of God.

Saints must examine this scenario to see if this is what they want. If the main body of LDS were to remain in Utah, which of course they would not, what would be the future of Utah, which is now so richly endowed with natural splendor? To accommodate the needs of such a burgeoning population would mean devastation of the fragile natural environment. Climatologically, most of Utah is a desert. By applying data provided by the Utah Governor's Office of Planning and Budget, we can see the calamity wrought by the Mormon rush to make spirit children mortals.

I was an environmentalist before I left high school—before the word was even conjured up. When I returned from upper Stoner Creek with my high school buddy, Jim Henry, at age fourteen in 1952, I knew the worth of wilderness. From the Abaho Mountains of Utah above Monticello, where I first taught high school, I could look across the southeast corner of Utah into Colorado, my boyhood state, and see the headwaters of Stoner Creek high in the San Juan Mountains.

Jim and I heard a rumor that if we walked a long ways up Stoner Creek, cutthroat trout were big and numerous. It was before the Wilderness Act but it was wilderness, really wild. Neither Jim nor I had been into the "backcountry." Nevertheless, early on a July morning, my dad delivered us at the mouth of Stoner Creek on the Dolores River, and we began the trek up the creek to investigate the rumor. It was true. That evening, after walking all day, we caught the large native fish from big, beautiful, black fishing holes.

It was wonderful, and nearly a lifetime later, I am telling the story again. Just before dark, we were walking back to our camp, totally satisfied and inspired with our decision to be there. We looked down from the trail to our campsite, perhaps one hundred feet below the trail near the steam bank. A herd of elk was standing in our camp, almost on our beds and camp gear. They didn't see us and we just watched—with goose bumps. They went on upstream and, in a couple of days, we went home to tell family and friends about our memorable experience.

It was about ten years later. I was working for the U.S. Forest Service in the Dolores District and the ranger, Bert Roberts, asked me to go to Stoner Mesa near the headwaters of Stoner Creek to survey for Engelmann spruce beetles. My mind was set for a pack trip when the ranger named the pickup truck I would drive. In the years since Jim Henry and I had hiked the trail to the backcountry of Stoner Creek, the Forest Service had opened Taylor Mesa and Stoner Mesa to logging. I followed the new road into Stoner Canyon and saw a bridge that crossed the creek.

A large trailer pulled by a pickup truck with a Minnesota license was parked near the bridge. From the bridge, the owner was looking downstream to where Jim and I had camped. I parked and looked over the habitat where my experience with the pristine land had occurred when I was a teenager. I walked over to where the owner of the trailer was standing, and the words he spoke will be with me for my lifetime. He said, "Isn't this the prettiest place you've ever seen?" It was still pretty, but relative to what? I could not give to my children or to my grandchildren the same experience of wilderness.

While I had been off to college, Alaska, and the army, Stoner country had been opened up to logging, as well as much other backcountry of the Dolores River drainage. It was supposed to supply timber for the Montolores Plywood Company. The U.S. government had decided that Montezuma and Dolores Counties of Colorado, San Juan County of Utah and San Juan County of New Mexico were economically depressed. Folks didn't have enough income. A large government grant, in combination with money from the local citizens, built the plywood plant to "spur" the economy. After only a few years of operation, it was discovered that the forest resources, even with the new millions of board feet of timber from the opened pristine forests, could not supply the plant. The project collapsed, and the empty mill sits atop the rim of the Dolores River Canyon where one can see all four states of the Four Corners Country.

The skeleton of the plywood plant should be left as a monument to poor natural resources planning. But most important, it would be a monument to the reckless taking of wild lands that are viewed by much of the public as worthless without development. In our transition from hunters and gatherers to farmers, and finally to city dwellers, we lost sight of our origin. For most of the time of our species, perhaps two hundred thousand years, we were hunters and gatherers in the wilderness, the wild lands. For much of the last eight thousand years, we have destroyed wild lands with enthusiasm. Just before we finished the job, we began to understand their value. Wetlands hold and purify water. They have great diversity of species. Forests keep the snow on the mountains and protect topsoil. And the interface of forests and meadows is habitat for wildlife that cannot exist without the two.

My high school science teaching associate and geologist in Monticello, Jeff Dowley, said that southern Utah was baldheaded geology. It didn't have the vegetation to cover the earth history that the visible strata show us. The geological processes and their manifestations in Utah are stunning to even those without geology education. But for those who can read the record in the rocks, it is a paradise: faults, volcanoes (some even geologically recent), volcanic necks, dikes, and sills that represent hundreds of thousands of acres where volcanoes poured out lava. There are limestone caves with stalactites and stalagmites.

The baldheaded geology of southern Utah is perhaps the earth's greatest exposure of past environments. They are represented in the sediments, one on top of another, that tell us of changes in the biosphere, that living layer of life on our planet. From the Uinta Mountains of northern Utah to the bottom of Grand Canyon, only thirty miles south of Utah in Arizona, is the astonishing history of the planet's life. There is record of life's beginning embedded in rocks at the bottom of the canyon that are at least two billion years old, ascending to our time, the Quaternary Period. Quaternary is the time in which we have become the dominant species with the ability to preserve or destroy the continuation of earth's diversity of life.

Most of Utah is desert and the southern Utah desert is the most spectacular desert that I know. As Chris Madson, editor of *Wyoming Wildlife* and recipient of National Wildlife Association's Conservation Achievement Award, said about the desert, "A refined taste in natural objects—that's what the desert requires of us. It hides its secrets in plain view, drifting on the wind, warming the evening light, changing the way we see. It is a place where the wild in us can run free. A place that sustains the spirit"[34] (Keynote address at the Red Desert Rendezvous, Rock Springs, Wyoming, June 18, 2011).

The Saints need to value and preserve the desert for it is holy in their faith. Moses and the Israelites of Old Testament time escaped to the desert and wandered forty years and purified themselves. Abraham and Sarah were commanded by God to find a new home in the desert. Jesus, in the New Testament, spent forty days in the desert in communication with God.

Wilderness may be defended with logic as I have often been called to do. But wilderness does not need logic for defense. It is like defense of one's children. As Chris Madsen said, "There are some things in life that simply aren't covered by logic. In fact, some of the very best things."

Life for me in Utah, intermittently 1958 through 1975, seemed always contentious with those who would see land for the dollars it would bring. That statement isn't completely honest. Wherever I have lived, when the value of wild lands is challenged, I am contentious. But in San Juan County, most of the local elected officials, and those elected to state government, always need a road to somewhere. The social studies teacher at the San Juan Junior High School, Rex Kinder, wanted his students to know local environmental issues, so he asked me to debate the Utah legislature representative of the county, the late Charles White, before his social studies classes.

White was the undisputed kingpin of San Juan County politics. He was an advocate of development and a leader of the "Sagebrush Rebellion," which challenged the federal government in the '60s and '70s for control of the public land. The stage was set and students wanted to see how their principal would fare with the leader of privatization of everything. Kinder said it was a draw. Well, I would say, not for me. Though the school administration brought down the population posters, the exponential population curves and data I used in the debate were difficult to challenge. Science won the day.

I remember Charles White's closing challenge, "We need people and development. We've picked with the chickens down here in this corner of the state long enough." He wanted development so the folks could make a "decent" living. Roads were needed to get the folks in to see and develop this land. Who would argue with a good living, but at the cost of what so many tourists came to see and value? The locals want to carve up San Juan County. They want roads to everywhere, like they had just discovered the auto. Here is what the National Trust for Historic Lands has to say about San Juan County and its "development."

> San Juan County in southeastern Utah is a stunningly beautiful area of high plateaus and deep canyons that contain the remains of at least 12,000 years of human history accessible to visitors and generally left in a natural state. The largest communities in the county—Bluff, Blanding and Monticello—are gateways to some of the most well known and heavily visited prehistoric pueblo and rock art sites and historic trails and settlements in all of Utah. In addition, the county is part of a much larger, incredibly rich prehistoric cultural landscape that spans the Four Corners area and includes places such as Canyons of the Ancients National Monument and Mesa Verde National Park in Colorado and Chaco Canyon in New Mexico.

> Unfortunately, many of the prehistoric and historic resources in San Juan County are being loved to death by a rapidly increasing number of national and international tourists, backpackers, off-highway vehicle (OHV) users and other recreationists. The Bureau of Land Management (BLM) Monticello Field Office— responsible for 1.8 million acres of land in the county—is under funded and understaffed and cannot keep up with archaeological site documentation, monitoring and stabilization, visitor education and law enforcement. Resultant problems include inadvertent damage to sites,

purposeful vandalism and looting, collapse of structures through benign neglect and creation of unauthorized, new walking and OHV trails that further expose sites to damage.[35] (preservationnation.org/issues/public-lands/bureau-of-land-management/san-juan-county.html)

Does this sound like more roads are needed? The topography of the Four Corners Country should best be left alone. The Spanish, the first ranchers, the Mormons, and the gold miners came there and met the Ute Indians and the Navajos. In retrospect, the area may have best become the world's largest national park. Here is a small list of the natural and cultural phenomena within a one-hundred-mile radius of the Four Corners Monument, the only place in the United States where four states have a common corner: the Ship Rock volcanic neck, Mesa Verde National Park, Arches National Park, Canyonlands National Park, Goose Necks of the San Juan State Park, Natural Bridges National Monument, Hoovenweep National Monument, the fourteen thousand foot peaks of the San Juan Range, the Dolores, Colorado, and the San Juan River canyons, the Abaho Mountains, the LaSalle Mountains, Edge of the Cedars State Park in Blanding, Monument Valley Navajo Tribal Park. The list has just begun.

The geology, ecology and evolution represented by the Four Corners are the greatest teaching resources that I know about. Geology has put our lives, our lifetimes, and our environmental sins into perspective. Geology asks if we know how long it takes to make a barrel of oil or a ton of coal. And evolution may be the most shortchanged concept in our school curriculum. The Four Corners Country is the world's greatest exposure of evolution. Students need concrete experiences to prepare them for this difficult concept.

Usually, in the ninth or tenth grade biology class, students learn that bacteria evolved over time to become elephants and great whales. What a huge abstract step to take. And evolutionary changes are not often related to the environmental changes represented by the geology. Regrettably, in the study of ecological relationships among organisms, the relationships are not related to students as the products of evolutionary processes over time. It is through evolution that the yuccas and moths are mutually dependent, and it is through evolution that bacteria live in our large intestine, and we regularly have gas in our stomachs. Evolution wedded these relationships. Evolution takes time, earth time.

At the San Juan Junior High School, I would lead students to the edge of town to clay soil above the Dakota Sandstone, and we would pick up brachiopod fossils, ones commonly called Devil's Toes. There were thousands of them. They are fossils of life that was in the saline seas one hundred and twenty million years ago, at least one hundred and eighteen million years before humans were on the earth.

What does that mean to Blanding and human existence there? Similarly, to illustrate the age of the earth relative to what I call "Super Market Time," in my secondary science teaching methods class at the University of Wyoming, the budding teachers would learn to carry out the activity called "Earth as a One-Year Movie," developed from an essay by James Rettie. To make well-informed decisions about actions that will affect the environment, it is important to understand time on a larger scale than personal human experience, or even historical time. Because many earth processes like oil and coal formation do not happen on a familiar human timescale but rather on a geologic timescale, it is important to understand the relationship between events happening on the scale of the age of the earth as opposed to the time resources such as coal and oil will last at the modern rate of consumption.

All earth citizens should know it has been only in the last two hundred years that humans have had the technology and population size to rapidly and dramatically affect the earth. For instance, today it takes 38 percent of earth's ice-free surface to feed seven billion people, and two billion more are expected by 2050. Geologic time is divided by geologists into eras, periods, and epochs. The Ice Age was the Pleistocene epoch. Our time may well be called the Anthropocene epoch, the geological age of humans. It is in this brief moment of earth's history that the human condition has changed dramatically, from daily subsistence, epidemics, and ignorance, to relative freedom from disease and some understanding of the earth systems that sustain life. Like evolution, the age of the earth and our effect on our planet should be primary to the curriculum.

To get a grasp of this concept, here is the activity, "Earth as a One-Year Movie"—quite condensed—as explained to preparing secondary science teachers at the University of Wyoming[36] ("Earth as a One-Year Movie," by Duane Keown and David Rizor, *Wild Wonderful Wyoming* [Secondary Activities Manual], University of Wyoming, 1998).

I'm hoping secondary teachers who may read this will add the activity to their curriculum.

>At the start of the activity, on a small slip of paper, an event in earth's history is given to each student, or small groups of students. Events are such things as: first cellular life, first photosynthesis, first dinosaurs, dinosaurs become extinct, Grand Canyon begins

to be cut in Arizona, first humans appear in Africa, Cro-Magnon people live in Europe, first pyramids are built by Egyptians, Birth of Christ, Declaration of Independence is signed. The time of these events may be "Googled" on the computer.

Outdoors is best for unrolling a 50-meter adding machine tape (50 meters is a little more than half a football field long). Have the students unroll the tape, and if it is a typical Wyoming day, they will need to put rocks on it to keep it from blowing away. Explain to them that the story you will read is called "Earth as a One-Year Movie," so you will need to have several students mark the time line off into equal 12-month segments. Forty-six meters is 4,600 millions of earth years, or 4.6 billion years, which is scientists' best estimate for the age of the earth. Have a student draw a "starting line" on the 50-meter tape and write "Formation of earth, 4.6 billion years ago." Divide the 46 meters of the tape into 12 even segments to represent the month of the year-long movie, beginning with January 1. At the end of December, have the students write today's year, AD 2012, and put a line across the tape at the end of December. Two millimeters back from this line draw another line across the tape.

Tell the students they have one task for the first part of the activity. They are to estimate when their event took place on the time line. They are to tape their selected time in earth's history that the event happened. After all events are placed, bring the group back together at the beginning of the tape. Read the introduction to Rettie's essay and then begin the walk to December 31, 2012, as you read the essay.

Below is the Introduction and James Rettie's essay, "Earth as a One-Year Movie."

Introduction

What if the whole history of earth, all 4.6 billion years, were recorded on a disk or as a movie film? Then, suppose we condense that very long tape so it would play the history in only one year. The condensed tape begins playing on December 31 at midnight and will play the whole history of earth in sequence in the 365 days that follow and end on December 31 at midnight a year later.

Earth as a One-Year Movie

Throughout the first few months of the film, the earth cools. There are no signs of life upon the earth until the end of February. Single-celled organisms appear first; by the end of May, many-celled life forms are evident. The Cambrian period, 600 million years ago, begins in the middle of November in our movie. Invertebrate animals are abundant in the ancient seas, and algae are the dominant plants. However, there is as yet no life on land. Near the end of November, plants make their first appearance on land, and in the oceans the first fishes appear. It is late November before the first air-breathing animals begin to invade the land. Terrestrial plants, abundant at this time, are unlike most vegetation that we know today. By early December, amphibians are well established, but it will be the middle of the month before reptiles evolve to begin their domination. The first half of December shows the time in earth's history known as the Carboniferous Period, when much of today's coal begins to form in the great swamps.

By December 12, dinosaurs have made their appearance; for a hundred million years, they reign (but less than nine days in the film, or one meter on our time line)

By December 20, they are gone; and we see the Rocky Mountains rising. Land plants begin to have flowers, and primitive mammals and birds resembling those of today are widespread. Modern forests are developing by December 23, and there is rapid diversification of mammals. It is after Christmas before the land that is now Arizona begins to rise, and the Colorado River starts to form the Grand Canyon.

The movie will last only a few more days, yet there have been no signs of human beings. It is December 31, at about eight o'clock in the evening, before the first human-like creatures venture onto the plains of Africa. At 10:00 p.m., ice invades from the polar regions of the planet; the most recent Ice Age has begun. The ice retreats and invades at least three more times before midnight. It is after 11:59 p.m. before human beings build their first cities. At 22 seconds before the end of the year, the Egyptians build their pyramids. At seven-tenths of a second before midnight, the Declaration of Independence is signed.

Why the mark two millimeters from the end of the tape that is December 31? The mark is two hundred thousand years before the present. Physical anthropologists believe it was about that time a species of the family Hominidae, genus *Homo*, evolved to be the species that is us, *Homo sapiens*, Latin for "wise man." We hope so. Was *Homo sapiens* the species that painted pictures on the walls of caves in southern France, the one we call Cro-Magnon, forty thousand years ago? Yes, and our species was around many generations before the Cro-Magnon tribes. Anatomically, modern-appearing humans originated in Africa about two hundred thousand years ago, reaching full behavioral modernity around fifty thousand years ago[37] ("Human Evolution by the Smithsonian Institution's Human Origins Program," *Human Origins Initiative*,

Smithsonian Institution). Cro-Magnon was only forty thousand years ago. That was 3.7 minutes from the end of a one-year movie, or about one-half of one millimeter on a forty-six-meter tape. Joseph Smith's history of North America began in the movie 14.3 seconds ago, and the Old Testament about the same as the pyramids, 22 seconds ago.

Understanding evolution and the age of the earth, based upon science, explains how we might treat earth and use its resources, as well as how we treat each other and our contemporary species. Chimpanzees and our DNA blueprints are nearly 99 percent identical. The 1 percent difference? Humans are distinct from chimpanzees in a number of important respects, despite sharing nearly 99 percent of their DNA. New analyses are revealing which parts of the genome set our species apart. The time element for the millions of species evolving and the relative time we are causing extinctions should alarm all earth citizens.

Knowing the time required in earth's history to produce the minerals, and especially fossil fuels, the carbon dioxide from which we pump into the atmosphere to cause global warming and climate change, is in the realm of Copernican science today. Across Wyoming, I give this example of how Wyoming relates to resources formation and climate change. The Cowboy State in 2008 exported more coal than the other top coal-producing states, Pennsylvania, West Virginia, and Kentucky combined, 462 million tons. In 1997, the state produced 200 million tons. No other state has ever produced 200 million tons in one year. In only ten years, the coal industry doubled the 1997 amount. Four hundred and sixty two million tons of coal in one-hundred-ton railcars end to end would reach around the earth twice at the equator. Based upon how long the coal will last, people may be oblivious to the numbers that are rarely published.

In 1997, the Wyoming State Geologist, Dr. Gary Glass, with the Wyoming Geological Survey stated that the best estimate for the life of Wyoming coal was between 400 and 500 years with the mining technology of that time. In 2008, the estimate for the life of Wyoming coal is less than half that of ten years ago, or 250 years. The technology of mining has improved. Will production double again in the next decade and leave 125 years of coal? Most Wyomingites hope so. It employs thousands and the coal industry sings its praises. But environmental education they do not have.

Most of the coal of Wyoming and Utah was formed in the late Cretaceous period and early Paleocene epoch. The Cretaceous period lasted from 145 million years ago until 65 million years ago, when dinosaurs became extinct. The Paleocene epoch spanned the interval between 65.5 million and 55.8 million years ago. It was a time when large areas of what are now the Rocky Mountains were lands with humid bogs and forests. For millions of years, plant materials accumulated and came under heat and pressure, finally forming coal. Wyoming ranks first in coal production, third in natural gas production, and sixth in oil production. It produces much more carbon that will go into the atmosphere as carbon dioxide, heat the atmosphere and cause climate change, than any of the U.S. states and most nations. Much like Wyoming, in Utah there is a rush to get the fossil fuels out of the ground. As Charles White would say, "So we can make a decent living." At what costs?

The problems caused by increased carbon dioxide in the atmosphere are difficult for laymen to comprehend and were for scientists for a very long time. A climatologist, Dr. James Hansen of NASA, who is recognized worldwide as the leading authority on greenhouse gases and their heating the atmosphere, says that politicians may sometimes compromise on political issues, but the laws of physics do not compromise. He fears that governments will not act soon enough on limiting greenhouse gas emissions in time to save our ecosystems and much of humanity. In the lead article, "Global Health Threats: Global Warming in Perspective" in the *Journal of American Physicians and Surgeons*, Fall 2009, the author, Indru Goklalny, says in introducing the article, "Influential policymakers have declared that climate change is one of the defining challenges of this century. In their wake, even august publications such as the *Lancet* have taken the position that "climate change is the biggest global health threat of the twenty-first century."[38]

This piece on global warming is added because the majority of Rocky Mountain legislators by their actions are in camp with the few global warming skeptics that remain. Among atmospheric scientists, skeptics are an extremely small minority. Especially in Wyoming, Idaho, and Utah political forces are strong against formation and enforcement of environmental regulations by federal agencies such as the Environmental Protection Agency, the Bureau of Land Management and the U.S. Fish and Wildlife Service. In Utah, the resentment of "feds'" interference with the state has a storied past.

Minimum government regulation appeals to Utah since the communities once endured severe government-sponsored oppression. But since the report by the United Nations' Intergovernmental Panel on Climate Change in 2007, the human activity relationship to heating the atmosphere that sustains us is near to Copernican science. Yet so much of our behavior disregards a sustainable environment, the one we evolved in. There is but one atmosphere we all share. Because of the environmental backlash in these states, environmental education is on the backburner of the stove. But there are positives happening.

What is Utah's wind energy resource potential? Utah has the technical potential to contribute nearly 2,500 megawatts of wind—this excludes sensitive lands, national parks, and areas unsuited for wind development. This amount of wind would provide enough energy for over 660,000 average Utah homes and yield a net economic benefit of approximately $2.7 billion and over 1,110 long-term jobs. These estimates are based on data from the National Renewable Energy Laboratory, the Utah State Energy Program, Utah Anemometer Data, Utah State University Jon M. Huntsman School of Business, and wind developers[39] (www. utahcleanenergy.org/clean_energy_101/wind_101#wind_potential, Utah Clean Energy). Along the Wasatch Front, the wind energy industry has taken off. With wind energy alone, 2,500 megawatts would supply all the Utah homes of 1980. But the population has doubled since 1980 and sustainable wind would not take care of the needs of Utah people.

Rock Port, Missouri, was the first town in the United States to be free of fossil fuels for its electricity, except for times the wind does not blow. It only has 1,500 people. The town has four large wind turbines that produce more electricity than its citizens use, and the town sells the surplus back into the grid, $68,000 worth last year. Rock Port can be the national model for small communities. Cheyenne is Wyoming's largest city, and all of its electricity on a regular windy day comes from Duke Energy's Happy Jack Wind Farm. The wind farm is five miles west of town. It has thirty-two turbines, and each will produce two million watts on a regular windy Wyoming day.

In Laramie, Wyoming, one of the coldest cities in the United States—that is cold in temperature, not socially—there is a passive envelope solar home built in 1981 that heats for zero dollars and no fossil fuels. It is two thousand square feet and was built by Vince and Joyce Sindt. It stays at a constant seventy degrees Fahrenheit, even when the temperature goes to forty below zero. In the solarium, the family raised its garden vegetables. Utah gets more days of sun than Wyoming. But what does sustainable living afford if human numbers continue to increase? If human numbers level out and energy consumption continues to follow a J curve, can we live sustainably with our environment? When I entered high school in 1951, the U.S. population was 151 million. In my lifetime, we have more than doubled our population. And Utah?

Back to Utah. We only had one family vacation when my two sisters and I were growing up. It was in 1953 to California to see my mother's brothers and sisters. A vacation for my folks was a trip to visit family. Yellowstone, Yosemite, those vacation sites weren't even considered. The first night was in Salt Lake, about three hundred miles from Cortez. Entering the Salt Lake Valley will always be memorable. Just to let you know how far in the woods Cortez was in 1953, we had not seen synthetic rubber cones that direct traffic on the highway. My dad, who was a horse and buggy driver before he drove a car, thought the cones would bounce up should we knock a few over. It was somewhere between Springville, Utah and Provo. We kids looked out the back window and told my dad, "They're not coming back up, Dad." For several miles we were on the alert for a siren.

The drive north to Salt Lake in the Utah Valley was exciting for us small-town folks. There was the anticipation of Salt Lake City. But first it was farms, maybe like Brigham Young had imagined it would be. North was to Spanish Fork, Springville, Provo, Orem, Pleasant Grove,

American Fork, and finally, Draper, then at the outskirts of Salt Lake City. There were miles and miles of small farms. It was August, and we could smell the newly cut hay. We could have stopped at a hundred fruit stands for all kinds of fresh homegrown fruit and vegetables before reaching Draper. The state had only seven hundred thousand people in 1950.

In the fall of 2010 the route to the Wyoming vs. BYU football game took us from Salt Lake City to Provo. The entire distance, forty-five miles, has become a megalopolis: motels, malls, apartment houses, supermarkets, all the stuff to supply people who make their living by ways other than farming. To see the changed land, Spanish Fork to Draper, I was taken back to my very first national conference after landing the professorial position at the University of Wyoming. It was the National Biological Science Teachers Conference at Anaheim, California in 1976 where I presented a new environmental education plan for Wyoming.

The day before the sessions began was for field trips, and the La Brea Tar Pits was my choice. From Anaheim to the tar pits is through Orange County and into downtown Los Angeles suburbia all of the way. The teacher beside me in the bus was a California high school biology teacher. He was pleasant, and we carried on polite conversation for the sixty miles' roundtrip. That was good because I was bored to look out the window and see miles and miles of exits, and the stuff covering pavement, like now extends between Provo and Salt Lake. Not wanting to be disparaging about the landscape that was the home state of my companion, I kept quiet. Finally, my seat partner broke the silence and said, pointing to our surroundings, "Look at it. Miles and miles of shit."

Of course it isn't shit. It is the stuff that all of those people use, the stuff to live and work there and to keep up with their neighbors. A few miles farther down the freeway, the bus driver over the speaker said, "Look to your right. There is the last orange grove of Orange County." The Utah Valley has become Los Angeles all over again. The main difference is that the Californians immigrated there, most of them over the last century. The Utah Valley is full into the surrounding mountains mainly with people who were born there. Two million, seven hundred thousand people live along the Wasatch Front. Today, daily across the apartments, shopping malls, and housing additions—mostly on asphalt—drifts the pollution of the metal foundries to the west and Bingham Canyon Mine. The mine is the world's largest man-made excavation. It is two and three-fourths miles across and three-fourths mile deep. It is so big that it can be seen from outer space.

Brigham Young's dream was an agrarian paradise—fruit and hay farms, flowers, and the land beautified in preparation for the second coming of Christ. Do the people know of his dream? Do they know why his dream went awry? It is far removed from the glorious Utah Brigham Young and his pilgrims entered in that time of misunderstanding. The first Utah prophet would roll over in his grave. The megalopolis, swollen by natural reproduction, draws down a society convinced that living in observance of their scriptures will lead them to the Promised Land. They may have reached that Promised Land in 1847.

Paul Hawken is a renowned entrepreneur, visionary environmental activist, and author of many books, most recently *Blessed Unrest: How the Largest Movement in the World Came into Being and Why No One Saw It Coming.* In May of 2009, he gave the commencement address at the University of Portland. This chapter ends with two excerpts from the beginning of his address. It is an ominous warning for Saints and all of us.

> This planet came with a set of operating instructions, but we seem to have misplaced them. Important rules like don't poison the water, soil, or air, and don't let the earth get overcrowded, and don't touch the thermostat have been broken.
>
> We need to figure out what it means to be a human being on earth at a time when every living system is declining.[40]

CHAPTER 6

INS AND OUTS

Navajo Indian Home

All the religions of the world, while they may differ in other respects,
unitedly proclaim that nothing lives in this world but Truth.

——Mohandas Gandhi

"Horse shit, Darrell! What kind of sheep dip operation went on in
the cafeteria at lunch today? We aren't preparing livestock for market.
We're supposed to be preparing these kids to be responsible, educated
American citizens. Skirt length and hair length don't have a damn

thing to do with it." It was my last year as San Juan Junior High School principal, 1974–1975. I was mad as hell.

The junior high and the senior high schools were part of the same complex in Blanding, Utah. The cafeteria was located in the high school, but it was shared by the junior high students. The event that had provoked my quick trip to visit Darrell Johnson, the high school principal, had occurred at the student entrance to the cafeteria at lunch. Darrell and some of the teachers had been enforcing the San Juan School District dress code.

At the doorway girls suspected of showing too much of their knees were forced to kneel to the floor to see if their skirt would touch the floor. Boys' hair was examined to see it didn't reach below their collars. A teacher measured while another wrote down the names of the guilty students. The boys in violation were almost entirely Indians who for centuries had customarily worn long hair. I had burned a path down the sidewalk to Darrell's office when an aide of his delivered a note to me suggesting that a long list of my students be suspended from school until they were ready to conform.

In the winter, some students from the north end of the Navajo reservation rode in their parents' cars and pickups for several miles before daylight to meet the San Juan School District bus in which they rode sixty miles one way to the junior high school or the senior high school in Blanding. There was one barber in Blanding, and the bus left at 3:30 p.m. to take the Navajo children home. There were no barbers between the homes of the Navajos and Blanding. Most of Navajo homes did not have electricity. Were the parents to cut their boys' hair with scissors and hand shears? The lack of electricity on the Navajo and Hopi reservations angers many of us who are familiar with the homes and communities of the people.

Beginning in 1968 at Black Mesa near Kayenta, Arizona, Peabody Energy mines from open pits the coal on the mesa that belongs to both Navajos and Hopis. Black Mesa coal goes to the Navajo Power Plant at Page, Arizona, where it generates electricity that goes to Las Vegas, Nevada; Los Angeles, California; Tucson, Arizona; and to the Central Arizona Project. In huge power lines, the electricity goes miles and miles past Navajo and Hopi homes that are without electricity. This appalling situation continues in 2012. All of the carbon from the coal goes into the atmosphere to cause global warming. I'm not sure if the principal, Darrell Johnson, was ever in a Navajo Hogan home. He just was not the type.

Dress codes and school efforts to enforce them were the unrelenting worry of school administrators in the 1960s and 1970s, but in Utah, especially those schools with gentile populations, a struggle waged continuously. In Blanding, the gentiles were almost entirely the Indians, and these nonconformers were to Mormons the descendants of Nephi's cursed brother Laman. The Nephite children were "white and delightsome," and the Mormons of Blanding added to the code, but not in writing, "conform with the dress of the Saints."

The history of rigid conformity to Mormon ways by the membership, and exclusion of those who don't, dates back to when Joseph Smith first gave Saints the rules of what it meant to be Mormon. But it was Brigham Young who put the barbs in the hooks. A short history is necessary to appreciate the cafeteria incident, because it will be seen that the lunchtime provocation of my disgust would have been very much the social order of the nineteenth and early twentieth century schools of Utah.

The Saints have been proselytizing the Native Americans since the church's beginning. If Indians join the church and go through the religious paces, they are back on the path from their predecessor's transgressions, and redemption will follow. It is redemption in this life for the sins of ancestors hundreds of years ago, until one day they will be "white and delightsome" according to their *Book of Mormon*. But in Blanding, the small percentage of Indians who joined the church were still on the outside, as I discovered one Sunday afternoon in the north end of Blanding while I was teaching science in Monticello. I first saw the Lamanite Branch.

San Juan County is what Aldo Leopold would have called rich land but poor land. Little of the county could be farmed, but it is rich in natural history. Sundays were our adventure days to see the natural phenomena, and my family and I were coming into Blanding from the northwest corner in our Dodge pickup when I saw another church. I thought the community had the one large and elegant church in the middle of the town. The other church was large and cheaply built of cinder blocks and painted white. My wife knew about it. It was the Lamanite Branch, plainly written on a white wooden sign, "Lamanite Branch of the Church of Jesus Christ of Latter-day Saints."

"You mean the Mormon Indians go to another church?" I asked her.

"That's right," she said.

In the early 1970s, while I was the principal of the junior high school in Blanding, the Mormon Church was having civil rights problems with blacks and on the Navajo reservation and in Blanding, with the American Indian Movement. The Navajos and Utes were beginning to make waves. Graffiti was beginning to appear on buildings in Blanding. The Navajos, and Utes on the much smaller White Mesa Reservation south of town, wanted a voice in the use of their resources, their schooling, and a part of the economy. Blanding Saints saw the smoke, and the Lamanite Branch was converted into a shirt factory for Indian employment.

I began my teaching career in Utah in 1960 at the Hideout Mine on the Deer Flat escarpment in San Juan County, Utah. It was curtain time at the Hideout Mine Elementary School, December 1960, and John Kennedy had just been elected. More people were gathered for the school's Christmas play than had ever met for any occasion in the whole Deer Flat region. There were perhaps sixty: parents, children, and others. The small Butler Steel Building, which had become the elementary school, was completely full of miners and family. The Christmas program wasn't supposed to draw more than the parents and the twelve school children; however, the metal structure was full, and folks were standing in the playground. Those who couldn't get in seemed to be content just to be at the gathering.

The Hideout Mine was located fifty-seven miles west of Blanding, where in 1960, only the first twelve miles of Highway 95, the principal route to the many uranium mines, were paved. The remaining forty-five miles to the mine were dirt road that wound through deep canyons, pinyon-juniper forest, up fascinating escarpments, and finally terminated at

Deer Flat, a half mile beyond the mine. At that time, the area was one of the most isolated regions within the contiguous forty-eight states. Before the discovery of uranium in the Schinarump formation, which outcrops for many miles on the Deer Flat escarpment, the country was only known to a few cowboys.

Let me retrace the path. I had found the Hideout when the Alaska money ran out at BYU. I registered for the third year to finish the bachelor of science degree, but after buying books, paying rent and tuition, there just wasn't enough money left. And I didn't want to be a full-time worker and a half-time student like it had been at Western State College. To be a full-time good student was the way for me to go to college. What I needed was another year like Alaska, isolated, where I could save money. So I checked out of BYU and headed for the Four Corners Country, my home range, where the Alaska job had begun and the oil and uranium booms were in full swing.

It was midafternoon as I decelerated the old Chrysler and rolled into Monticello. I would be back in Cortez in a little more than an hour, but without a job. At the Y and in Cortez, I had heard that the San Juan School District in Utah was having a difficult time finding teachers for its most isolated schools. The whole county of eight thousand square miles comprised only one school district; by land area it was the largest school district in the United States. I had not arrived at Monticello, the county seat of San Juan County, when I had the impulsive idea that I might teach at one of those way-out-yonder schools. The names of Fry Canyon, Hite, and LaSalle in the county were familiar mining activity names, but where was the Hideout Mine? That was my thought as Ben Donan, assistant superintendent of San Juan School District, was about to explain. He couldn't be very specific because he hadn't been there.

The Hideout Mine was way off the beaten path and there were about a dozen students needing a teacher.

Ben Donan said that if I wanted the job, it would probably be mine. I would need a provisional teaching certificate since I wasn't, by state standards, qualified to teach the elementary grades. My credentials were my good college record, and I am sure in Mormon country, two years at BYU was in my favor. He asked whom I could give for a character reference. I had told him I went to school in Cortez, Colorado, sixty miles to the east, but before I could name a reference, he told me he knew Ike Woods, principal of the Cortez high school. He would call Principal Woods.

The following Monday morning at my folks' home in Cortez, the phone rang, and Ben Donan was on the line. He said I could be the first teacher at the Hideout. He said he talked with Ike Woods. Woods said he didn't know what kind of a teacher I might be, but I was a "damn good baseball player." He told me that Ludwig Koch, superintendent of the Hideout, would be at his office at 5:00 p.m. that day, and I could ride with him or follow his pickup with my car to the mine. Late that afternoon with several boxes of books, pencils, and tablets in the bed of his pickup, the mine superintendent and I headed for the Hideout. It was dark when we arrived at the rim of White Canyon, and Ludwig stopped and pointed out the lights of the mine operation across the canyon. "It doesn't look far," he said. "But we have to go way up the canyon to get there. It's seventeen miles." The last seventeen miles took an hour. I need not describe the condition of the road.

When we reached the mine, Ludwig, a native of Germany who had recently completed a master's in mining engineering at the University of Utah, stopped his pickup in front of a Butler Steel Building. As he got out of the pickup, he said, "This will be the school. I've got to tell a couple of miners in there that they'll need to move out in the morning." The building was perched on a cutout space in the slope that went into White Canyon. He knocked on the door, and two dark-complexioned guys came to the door. Ludwig called them by name, apologized, and in a joking manner told them their home was to become the school. I later learned they were from Greece and had been classmates of his in Salt Lake City at the university. The superintendent told me I could live with him, but his wife-to-be would soon be moving to the trailer home where he lived. He said there was a room in the school where I could live. Sight unseen, I chose the schoolroom.

I slept that night on a couch in Ludwig's mobile home that was parked about a hundred yards south of the school building in another carved-out shelf on the White Canyon rim. After breakfast the next morning Ludwig took me around to meet the families that had been hoping for a teacher. There were only six, with a total of twelve children to send to the new school. Ludwig asked the mothers to help clean the bachelor's home that had been appropriated for the school.

The building was about twenty-five by thirty-five feet. It had only one large room and a small room, where I would live, about twelve feet by ten feet partitioned off as a kitchen with a twin bed and closet. That afternoon, Ludwig and I gathered up about two dozen empty wooden powder boxes near the portal of the mine to use for seats and desks in the school until the school district truck arrived later in the week with supplies. By midafternoon the school was clean with no signs of the lifestyle of the bachelors. The bathroom for the students and the teacher was an outhouse about two hundred feet from the school with a magnificent view of White Canyon, but no flush.

At the end of the week, the school truck arrived with desks, more books, a chalkboard, a tetherball stand, and a basketball hoop. A passenger in the truck was a late middle-aged lady, Rita Dailey, who became a grand friend of mine as well as my supervisor. She was delightful. She knew the difficulties of the county school system, the problems no amount of money could solve, even though the county had plenty. They had given me a bonus to go to the remote Hideout site. She knew the educational difficulties of transient miners and their children and the added problems of gentiles in Utah. They did most of the mining. She was a Mormon. Her son, Garry Dailey, later in Monticello became my associate science teacher and a close friend.

The student body consisted of three first graders, four second graders, a fourth grader, a fifth grader, a seventh grader, and two eighth graders. Just making a living for their families was the objective of the miners, and religion or religious sacrifices were of little concern. At least three of the families were Jack Mormons, all with children in the school. In addition to their infrequent association with the LDS Church, Jack Mormons I have known drink coffee, smoke cigarettes, and drink whiskey. Outside the conforming pressures of that religious order, their language and habits make them seem in rebellion against their pronounced faith, but that may be a hasty judgment. Their religion is Mormonism, they believe Joseph Smith was a prophet of God, and they see themselves as black sheep. They defend their church and would want a Mormon funeral.

Many of the miners of the Hideout were gentiles and could trace their

Utah mining heritage. Nearly all communities of Utah began around agriculture, and Saints owned the arable land. What was left for the oversupply of children from the farms and newer immigrants to Utah was mining. It paid well. It became the employment that was associated with gentiles and Jack Mormons.

The early agrarian–mining relationship continued on in the new mining boom of southeastern Utah. It was not unlike the relationship with the Park City area and older mines in the nineteenth century. The finding of silver, gold, and lead sparked the first silver mines in Park City in the 1860s. Near Bingham, Utah, it was copper. Mormons in their towns sold the grubstake to the miners, including liquor, cigarettes, and coffee. But in all of San Juan County, all eight thousand square miles of it, there were only two outlets for liquor. There was the Blue Goose Saloon in Monticello and across the street a liquor store.

Monticello has an acceptance of gentiles and Jack Mormons. Its society and relationship with gentiles is typical of towns at the periphery of Utah that interface the non-LDS world. The gentile pinto bean farmers and wheat farmers of Dolores County, Colorado, trade in Monticello. Some are relatively wealthy. The Blue Goose Saloon in Monticello has a long history. Most of the locals can sing a verse or two of the county's favorite historical song that mentions the old saloon. The song is called "Blue Mountain," the local name for the Abahos. It is about a lonely gentile cowboy in San Juan County in the early ranching days. I lived in the county long enough to know all of the song. Here's the start and the bit about the Blue Goose Saloon.

> My home it was in Texas, my past you must not know,
> I seek a refuge from the law, where the sage and pinion
> grow.

Chorus
Blue Mountain, you're a-zure deep, Blue Mountain with
sides so steep, Blue Mountain with horse-head on your side,
you have won my love to keep. (On the east side of the mountain,
spruce, fir and meadows form a vivid horse's head)
....
....
I chum with Lad-die-go Gordon, I drink at the Blue-Goose Saloon.
I dance at night with the Mor-mon girls and ride home be-neath the moon.

The Utah state government has always tightly controlled the sale of liquor, and in the 1960s, it was more controlled than in the twenty-first century, which saw the Winter Olympics of 2002 liberalize considerably alcohol sales in the Mormon state. In the twentieth century, there was no advertising of liquor sales. In 1960, purchasing liquor was like buying prescription drugs. The bottles and cans were behind a counter that the patron stepped to for the purchase. In those days, it wasn't even displayed. Many of the Hideout miners would not buy their groceries, cigarettes or liquor from the Mormons. They drove the additional sixty miles—eighty-two miles from Blanding—to Cortez, Colorado. And Cortez had nightspots that were hopping in the boom years. Though Blanding sold cigarettes and coffee to the Jack Mormons and gentiles, no liquor was sold in Blanding. It has always been dry.

Utah is the Mormon state with a highly organized church structure that continues to radiate into government and education. It isn't the theocracy Brigham Young founded but the greatest organized power in Utah remains the LDS Church. The Navajos, the Utes, or the Hideout miners were not part of the church structure. The miners did have a very loosely organized society. The night of the school's Christmas party, the society met and prepared to have a good time.

At the Hideout school, the curtains (the two dark-blue blankets from my bed) were drawn, and the play began. The crowd loved it! But the play, including some group singing of Christmas carols, only lasted about forty-five minutes. It just couldn't be over—and it wasn't.

Leman May, the straw boss at the mine, was a good lead guitar player, and the Whitely brothers brought their guitars. I play several instruments. That night, it was the trumpet and guitar. About a month before at Leman's birthday party, we learned we could begin and end a song together. I guess we were satisfactory. Leman hollered, "Let's dance." The people pulled the desks and chairs back, and with little reluctance, the mining community was dancing. Some had noticed earlier that Swede, a likeable upper middle-aged miner, had left early. But about the time the dance began, he was back in his pickup with a few cases of beer from his cache on the cool north side of his cabin. His leaving before the ending of the play and the singing was a clue, but not to me, that the dance and party was not completely spontaneous.

The Christmas party was not the usual Utah school gathering. In the sixties and through the seventies, school functions began and ended with a prayer. That night we played every song that Leman, the Whitleys, and I knew, and a few we didn't know: "Your Cheating Heart," "Please Release Me," Bob Wills's "San Antonio Rose." I remember how "The Beer Barrel Polka" got everyone dancing.

It was late in the dance that I went into my partitioned room for some reason that I have long since forgotten; however, on my bed was a sight that will not be forgotten. Several small babies were lying side by side like cordwood, crosswise, the full length of my bed. The stage curtains—my blankets—were placed neatly over them, and there wasn't a stir. That they were able to sleep through "The Beer Barrel Polka" and "When the Saints go Marching In" was testimony to the disruptive lives those little children knew. I don't know if the San Juan School board or the school superintendent ever knew of the merriest Christmas program ever in a San Juan school. If they had, I might not have been a science teacher later in Monticello or for sure not a Blanding school principal. But it was not my school building or the school district's either. It wasn't the dancing. Mormons love to dance. Their objection would have been the beer.

The miners were my kind of people. I was born in the family home in the Colorado gold mining town of Rico. My dad was a miner turned county treasurer. His baseball batting laurels got him elected, not his tenth grade education. Dolores County voters believed he was the best batter on the Montezuma–Dolores Counties All Stars team. But his ability to keep track of the beans for Dolores County, even through the Great Depression, got him elected time after time for fourteen years until we left for Cortez in Montezuma County. We moved when county officials decided the courthouse should be in the then prospering town of Dove Creek.

———————

How Mormons became religiously and socially separated from America is a long and complicated story. Earlier, we examined their beginnings and theological ideas that isolated the body of followers. It is difficult for historians to retrace the events, the state of mind of the participants, and the synergistic effects of multiple events that led to the condition of Mormonism when it reached Utah in 1847. Or the lingering effects today of the events of Midwestern conflicts, the hardships in the wilderness of the Territory of Deseret, and the attitudes, aspirations, and disappointments with the failure so far in establishment of the Kingdom of God. There is virtue here. They are a tough, hardy, dedicated people.

Restaging the reality and the atmosphere that led to the condition of present-day Utah is impossible. The effort to do this shows the bias of the historian perhaps more than any other event in American history. If the historian is an active Latter-day Saint, the events are approached with the foregone conclusion that Joseph Smith was a prophet of God, and with the prophet's direction, the people were carrying out the will of their God. There are many more historians on the LDS side of the fence than the other where the historians often have an axe to grind.

Events that separated me from the Saints while in Utah were real and personal. The late Mormon psychologist, philosopher, and sociologist, Ephraim Edward Erickson, produced the first objective look at the evolution of the sentiment of the Utah Latter-day Saints toward gentiles. He became a professor at the University of Utah. His study was divided into three parts: (1) the conflict of the church with gentiles from its beginning; (2) the struggles to preserve and build a stable society in the Rocky Mountains; and (3) the relinquishing by the church of much of its temporal authority, and its growing concern and effort to control the spiritual lives of its members in the face of science, gentile influences, and the democratization of the Mormon theocracy.

Erickson believed that the basis of the conflict with their neighbors throughout the Midwest was because of the Saints' indifference to the non-Mormons that surrounded them. He says that in some locations, early in the church history, they were driven out for "minding their own business." They were preoccupied with building Zion; their business was distinct from the gentiles, with the exception of those who joined the Mormon Church. Erickson says, "Two peoples cannot live together unless there is some common ground, some natural interest or condition for cooperation. It is a vital principle in human society that, 'he who is not for us is against us.' Human nature cannot tolerate indifference"[41] (*The Psychological and Ethical Aspects of Mormon Group Life*, p. 28, The University of Utah Press, 1975). Certainly, Erickson's study reflects the history of the Mormon establishments across the Midwest and into the Rocky Mountains and isolating factors. But there is more.

Mormon rituals isolate them and kit them together. I look back at the testimony meetings at BYU. Public profession of faith is a particularly significant aspect of Mormon ritual. It is more common and regular than with most denominations. Secret rituals bind them together. In the sacred temples, the rituals are very secret. They are administered to a selected group. The secrets weld the sharers into a special group. And through temple ceremonies, the most righteous receive their garments that are worn where they are not seen by the public, unlike outer signals like the kippah (skullcap) that identifies Jewish males.

But why did they ignore and disrespect other religions to the degree they would not associate? It comes from the "first vision" of Joseph Smith when God told him that all religions on earth are an abomination in his sight. Not very nice language for describing others' religions.

Why must so many religions believe theirs is the only "true" religion? I reflect on the Taliban disrespect for other religions in 2001 when it was world news that the Taliban in Afghanistan had destroyed the Buddhas of Bamiyan, giant statues of Buddha carved into the cliffs of Bamiyan Valley in the sixth century. The statues are 140 miles northwest of Kabul. They were intentionally dynamited in March 2001 by the Taliban, on orders from leader Mullah Mohammed Omar, after the Taliban government declared that they were "idols." International opinion strongly condemned the destruction of the Buddhas that represented so much more than the Buddha.

History is replete with religious leaders declaring theirs to be the true religion and destruction of the icons of other religions, and even the taking of lives of those who will not practice and acknowledge the religion imposed upon them as the only true faith. My recent trip to Peru and visit to the Machu Picchu ruins of the Incas helped put the Mormons and their "only true religion" pronouncement into perspective with the world's religious history and intolerance that continues today. Incas worshiped their sun god and other nature gods. They considered their king, the Sapa Inca, to be the "child of the sun." The Incas inflicted their religion upon most of South America. They built temples and monuments to their gods using the most tortuous and exacting stone masonry ever accomplished, even to be declared the seventh wonder of the world. In the 1500s came the Spanish looking for gold, and padres with them to sanctify their exploitations, and impose Catholicism on the Inca nation and nearly all of Central America. The Incas with their religion were to the Spanish heretics. Their sun god and nature gods were the wrong gods. The Spanish built elaborate churches across South America and Central America to worship their Christian god. The Christian god the Spanish worshipped was, to them, the true god.

Interestingly, the Andes Mountains represent the eastern edge of the Pacific plate induction zone, and the whole region is earthquake prone. The Inca temples, which are protected from destruction as national monuments today, will probably outlive the Catholic temples. Inca temples were built with such exact masonry techniques they withstand the most violent quakes while the Catholic temples often crumble.

Wherever the Mormons accumulate members, they build their temples to carry out the most sacred rituals: marriages, baptism of the dead, and other rites they call "temple work." It took forty years of cutting granite stone from the Wasatch Mountains of Utah to build the Salt Lake Temple. Worldwide, there are more than 130 extravagant Mormon temples. How little religious practices change over time in the name of the gods that are the only true god. Religious minorities invariably suffer a loss of freedom in those countries that do not have a wall of separation between government and religion. Let us recognize and rejoice in our First Amendment.

––––––

It is no wonder that when the Mormons reached Utah to escape their persecution in the Midwest, the world beyond their society was to them the world led by the devil, for it had behaved hellishly. Another revelation to Joseph Smith justified for them that the Lord was their God and the devil was the god of the gentiles. It was in *Doctrine and Covenants,* Section 1:35–36. "The devil shall have power over his dominion... And also the Lord shall have power over his Saints and shall reign in their midst and shall come down in judgment upon... the world."[42]

This chapter does not deal with the conflicts in the Midwest, except to say the time in Ohio, Missouri, and Illinois embittered the Saints to the extent that when they left Nauvoo, Illinois, in 1846, hate for the gentiles is not an abhorrent enough descriptor to paint the feeling for the enemy they left. Culmination was their violence, but not the culmination of vengeance, in the Mountain Meadow Massacre that occurred in 1857. The following account of this horrid event is taken from Wikipedia.org; *The Mountain Meadows Massacre* by Juanita Brooks, 1950; and *Blood of the Prophets* by Will Bagley, 2002.[43]

> The Mountain Meadows massacre was a series of attacks on the Baker–Fancher emigrant wagon train, at Mountain Meadows in Southern Utah. The attacks culminated on September 11, 1857, in the mass slaughter of an emigrant party by the Iron County district of the Utah Territorial Militia and some local Indians.
>
> The wagon train, composed almost entirely of families from Arkansas, was bound for California on a route that passed through the Utah Territory during a turbulent period later known as the Utah War. After arriving in Salt Lake City, the Baker–Fancher party made their way south, eventually stopping to rest at Mountain Meadows. While the emigrants were camped in the meadow, nearby militia leaders including Isaac C. Haight and John D. Lee made plans to attack the wagon train. Intending to give the appearance of Indian aggression, their plan was to arm some Southern Paiute (Pah Vant) Indians and persuade them to join with a larger party of militiamen, disguised as Indians, in an attack.
>
> During the initial assault on the wagon train, the emigrants fought back, and a five-day siege ensued. Eventually, fear spread among the militia's leaders that

some emigrants had caught sight of white men, and had probably discovered who their attackers really were. This resulted in an order by militia commander William H. Dame for the emigrants' annihilation. Running low on water and provisions, the emigrants allowed a party of militiamen to enter their camp who assured them of their safety and escorted them out of their hasty fortification. After walking a distance from the camp, the militiamen, with the help of auxiliary forces hiding nearby, attacked the emigrants. Intending to leave no witnesses of Mormon complicity in the attacks, and to prevent reprisals that would further complicate the Utah War, the perpetrators killed all the adults and older children (totaling about 120 men, women, and children). Seventeen children, all younger than seven, were spared.

Following the massacre, the perpetrators hastily buried the victims, leaving their bodies vulnerable to wild animals and the climate. Local families took in the surviving children, and many of the victims' possessions were auctioned off. Investigations, temporarily interrupted by the American Civil War, resulted in nine indictments during 1874. Of the men indicted, only John D. Lee was tried in a court of law. After two trials, Lee was convicted and executed. He chose the firing squat, a form of execution still used in Utah today. Historians attribute the massacre to a combination of factors including both war hysteria and strident Mormon teachings. Scholars still debate whether senior Mormon leadership, including Brigham Young, directly instigated the massacre or if responsibility lies with the local leaders of Southern Utah. Brigham Young was complicit in blaming the massacre on the Paiute Indians, according to Lee. He met with Brigham Young, and Young insisted that he write a report of the incident and blame the Indians. The report was a test of Lee's obedience. He wrote the report and blamed the Paiutes. But there were too many witnesses, though the murderers swore to never tell the story of the massacre. When the investigation began, Brigham Young went with U.S. Judge Cradlebaugh into southern Utah for arrests, but the dozens of perpetrators were not to be found. Nineteen years after the massacre, John D. Lee paid with his life. But before his execution, he told the story in detail.

It was the most distressing event ever in Utah by Mormons, and it enraged a nation that was suspicious of their American loyalty. In the Midwest, Joseph Smith and his brother's murder in the Carthage, Missouri, jail by a mob was the impetus for the move by the church to Utah. They had become martyrs. In multiple events before their prophet's murder, in the Midwest settlements, the Saints' crops were burned by the gentiles, temples and homes were burned, and Mormon lives were taken. But multiple wrongs do not make a right. To explain is not to excuse.

Today, the Mountain Meadow Massacre is recognized by descendants of the victims and the perpetrators of the crime. In 1988, the Mountain Meadows Association, composed of descendants of both the Baker–Fancher party victims, and the Mormon participants, designed a new monument in the meadow. This monument was completed in 1990 and is maintained by the Utah State Division of Parks and Recreation. In 1999, the Church of Jesus Christ of Latter-day Saints replaced the U.S. Army's cairn, and the 1932 memorial wall with a second monument, which it now maintains by the church.

The early Mormons viewed the gentiles as misled—rather than evil—as lost and in need of the discovery of the original Christianity that they would offer the world. They believed it was a utopian society, and its members' view of society was one of generosity, extending to the outside world a new light, a home in Zion. But sixteen years into the experiment in the Rocky Mountains, the people had come to hate outsiders. Thomas Stenhouse, editor, writer, and a very astute early Mormon, described the change that he observed in Mormonism:

> No faith could be more liberal than written Mormonism. In the beginning of its mission it was a beautiful ideal… In creed writing they are broadly cosmopolitan in sentiment, warmly inviting to "fair freedom's feast," away up in the Rocky Mountains… but when once the Plains have been traversed, there the reception of… the religious stranger have been like the chilling breezes of the frigid zone… In intercourse with mankind (Mormonism) is the trampled worm still in agony, the remembrance of "persecution" that every forward, generous impulse and withers the soul with the baneful teaching that "he who is not for us is against us."… No professor of religion… could be more bitterly bigoted than the rigidly orthodox among the Mormons today.[44] (*The Rocky Mountain Saints*, T. H. B. Stenhouse, p. XXII, Appleton & Company, 1873)

The Mississippi Valley of Missouri and Illinois is some of the richest farmland in the world. I remember a town in Illinois across from Hannibal, Missouri, where a sign at the town entrance read, "We Can Grow Anything." It was so humid I wondered about humans. But the corn in August was eight feet tall. If there ever was a Garden of Eden, it may have been along the Mississippi. And of course that is what Joseph Smith told his Saints, that it began for all of us somewhere near Independence, Missouri. It was the biblical Garden of Eden.

The feeling of the Mormon pioneers as they began to plow the arid Salt Lake Valley, knowing the character of the land they were forced to abandon, and not knowing if the dry Great Basin soil would even nurture their Midwestern crops, must have fueled fires of resentment lingering in the hearts of the Saints. For two years, the Utah Mormons were threatened with starvation, and the journey across half of the continent had cost them many lives. An aftertaste of those years of maladjustment in the wilderness remains with the Saints today, but to understand the feelings of the time toward the gentiles, listen to the words of their leader, Brigham Young:

> We do not intend to have trade or commerce with the gentile world, for so long as we buy from them, we are in a degree dependent upon them. The Kingdom of God cannot rise independently of the gentile nations until we produce, manufacture, and make every article of use, convenience, or necessity among our own people... I am determined to cut every thread of this kind and live free and independent, untrammeled by any of their detestable customs and practices.[45] (Quote from *The Mormon Experience,* Leonard J. Arrington and Davis Bitton, p. 122, Alfred A. Knopf, 1979)

Under Brigham Young's direction, in the Utah wilderness, the Mormons were at last free to live the grand design of the restored early Christian society that Joseph Smith had revealed to them. Their god was the God of Israel. Smith's revelations reaffirmed that they were the chosen, and God would punish their oppressors. "Let all the Saints rejoice, therefore, and be exceedingly glad, for Israel's god is their God, and He will mete out a just recompense of reward upon the heads of all their oppressors"[46] (*Doctrine and Covenants,* Section 127:3).

Survival in the Utah wilderness required a total group effort. Mormons depended upon Mormons. One man could not divert a river and channel it down a canal onto the farmlands. One family could not build a temple or set up a community. In the new Kingdom of God, it was required that the individual merge with the group which resulted in loss of individual identity. The canal, the temple, the church were most important. Erickson said of a Mormon's personal life, "His entire life became identified with his group. The self was a group self; it was made up of the combined interests of all the brethren. When they suffered, he suffered in a very real sense." The beehive and word "industry" became the official motto and emblem for Utah on March 4, 1959. The early pioneers had few material resources at their disposal and therefore had to rely on their own industry to survive. The beehive was chosen as the emblem for the provisional State of Deseret in 1848 and was maintained along with the word "industry" on the seal and flag when Utah became a state in 1896. But in the Mormon faith, after a life of toil for the success of the group, the individual must still face judgment day by himself or herself.

In Utah, the stage was set for the rigid theocracy that Mormonism became. Many adherents had come from Europe to help build Zion. That was the goal in preparation for the second coming of Christ. In the new Zion, there was little dissention. Everyone's goal was the same. Jesus was coming soon, and the New Jerusalem must be made ready to receive him. The organization was, and still is, phenomenal.

Isolation in the Great Basin wilderness discouraged dissenters from conflict with the prophet or actually leaving the body of the faithful. In the desert wilderness, what was there for the dissenter or the apostate? In the Midwest, there were people of European culture in the surroundings.

In the new Zion, there were the Indians. Apostatize and live with the Lamanites? Not hardly.

The theocracy needed a leader, and it found it in Brigham Young. He had successfully led them eleven hundred miles by foot to look into the Utah Valley where, legend has it, that he said, "This is the place." Preparation for the big event began. In 1866, nineteen years after their arrival, William H. Dixon, the famous British travel writer of the American West, paid a visit to Salt Lake City. Excerpts from his impressions one hundred and forty-five years ago help us to understand today the changes Utah society has undergone and the fanaticism of Mormons early in their Utah history.

> Strange as the new sectarians may seem to us, they must have in their keeping some grain of truth. They live and thrive, and men who live by their own labor, thrive by their own enterprise, cannot be all together mad. Their streets are clean, their houses bright, their gardens fruitful. Peace reigns in their cities. Harlots and drunkards are unknown among them...

> As they state their case, Abraham is their perfect man; who forsook his home, his kindred, and his country, for the sake of God. Sarah is their perfect woman; because she called her husband lord, and gave her handmaiden Hagar into his bosom for a wife. Everything that Abraham did they pronounce as right for them to do; all gospels and commandments of the Church, all laws and institutions of man, being void and of no effect when quoted against the practices of that Arab sheikh. Putting under his feet both the laws of science and the lessons of history, they preach the duty of going back, in spirit and in name, to the priestly and paternal form of government which existed in Syria four thousand

years ago; casting from them, as so much waste, the things that all other white men have learned to regard as the most precious conquests of time and thought... personal freedom, family life, change of rulers, right of speech, concurrence in laws, equality before the judge, liberty of writing and of voting. They cast aside these conquests of time and thought in favor of Asiatic obedience to a man (Brigham Young) without birth, without education, whom they have chosen to regard as God's own vicar on the earth. No pope in Rome, no czar in Moscow, no caliph in Baghdad, ever exercised as much power as the Mormons have conferred in Young. "I'm one of those men," said Elder Stenhouse... perhaps the man of highest culture whom we saw in Salt Lake City... who thinks that brother Brigham ought to do everything; he has made this church, and he ought to have his way in everything. A man had better go to hell at once," said Stenhouse, "if he cannot meet Brigham's eyes.[47] (*New America*, Willliam H. Dixon, pp. 171–173, J. B. Lippincott & Co., 1869)

After the establishment of the Saints in Utah, the church provided the means by which a steady stream of Europeans could emigrate to Zion. This was the Perpetual Immigration Fund, established in 1849, to which the Saints contributed millions. One only need look in a Salt Lake City phone book, or walk down the streets of a Utah town, to discover the countries that contributed the most people to the new kingdom. Most were Britons and Scandinavians. They were mostly poor in finances and education. There were also some French and Italian immigrants. The steady stream of immigrants to Utah, and then to the other Latter-day Saint communities during the second half of the nineteenth century was an important factor in strengthening their hold on available lands. In the priesthood-controlled communities, there was little incentive for nonmembers to join the community, unless they wanted to join the church, for the control of the community rested within the church. By the turn of the nineteenth century, much of the arable farmland of the Rocky Mountains was filled with Saints, but even more was owned by gentiles, and the literal concept of the gathering of Israel, although a cornerstone of the faith, was allowed to slowly fade away.

Today, there is the shadow of the Kingdom of God within Utah and regions of the states that surround it. LDS influence by no means ends where the Utah border ends. In western Wyoming, southern Idaho, and northern Arizona especially, Mormons prevail, but with little assistance from state governments.

Since the changes were made to allow Utah to join the union, such as abandonment of polygamy, other changes to accommodate American pluralism have come, but slowly and painfully. This was my experience while in Zion: three years at BYU and ten in San Juan County. The main impediment is scriptures carved in stone by the first prophet and founder of the faith. What does it mean to be human? It is dynamic. We were centuries in abandonment of slavery, and the institution seems unimaginable today.

Wyoming was the first state to allow women to vote, and today, they head giant corporations. This is not to say we have overcome the bigotry and prejudice that stymie equality of ethnic groups and women. But in Mormonism, and in other faiths, scriptures slow the climb or at times stop the progress. Abandonment of subservient roles of women in the LDS Church and total acceptance of gays and lesbians may be the next civil rights issue that will require more revelations for LDS survival. The Saints want to be saints and do right by humanity, but they just keep running into those scripture roadblocks.

The LDS Church with 14 million members cannot ignore the intellectual undertow within the church that come from organizations that challenge the theology and church decisions anchored in scriptures that will not fit our times. The most important of these is *Dialogue: A Journal of Mormon Thought*. It is the oldest independent journal in Mormon Studies. *Dialogue* was originally the creation of a group of young Mormon scholars at Stanford University led by Eugene England and G. Wesley Johnson. *Dialogue*'s original offices were located at Stanford. The first issue appeared in the spring of 1966, and during its first few years, the editorial board and staff came to include many notables in the subsequent history of the Church of Jesus Christ of Latter-day Saints. *Dialogue* has, nevertheless, remained totally independent of church auspices over the years, thanks to loyal readers and the generosity of its donors. The editorial boards have been composed mainly of scholars and lay writers who are participating members of the LDS Church. For obvious reasons, they are often labeled social Mormons—they can't break the church habit. It is the society that holds them. It is their society too, and for most, since birth.

Literally half of the members of the Church of Jesus Christ of Latter-day Saints are technically out of the church. These are the women; they are the "outs" that are "in." Women are excluded from roles of true authority by the literal interpretation of Mormon scriptures. By revelation, only males can hold the holy priesthood, the authority from their God to govern the church. Sonia Johnson, a Mormon woman who was excommunicated from the Church, wrote the book, *From Housewife to Heretic* in 1981. She said about the priesthood, "It is the sacred… the masculine glue that holds the world together."[48] Church officials do not see it different. Go to the official website of the Mormon Church and ask the question, "Why don't women hold the priesthood in the Mormon Church? How do women lead in the Mormon Church?" Gordon B. Hinckley, the fifteenth president of the Church of Jesus Christ of Latter-day Saints from 1995 until his death in 1997, answered the questions.

> Women do not hold the priesthood because the Lord has put it that way. It is part of His program. Women have a very prominent place in this Church. Men hold the priesthood offices of the Church. But women have a tremendous place in this Church. They have their own organization. It was started in 1842 by the Prophet Joseph Smith, called the Relief Society, because its initial purpose was to administer help to those in need. It has grown to be, I think, the largest women's organization in the world... They have their own offices, their own presidency, their own board. That reaches down to the smallest unit of the Church everywhere in the world...
>
> The men hold the priesthood, yes. But my wife is my companion. In this Church, the man neither walks ahead of his wife nor behind his wife but at her side. They are co-equals in this life in a great enterprise.[49] (www.mormon.org/faq/women-in-the-church/-Cached, website of the LDS Church)

Hinckley described the role of women but he did not deny males hold the roles of authority. Are they really co-equals?

Authorities of Mormondom tell women continuously how important they are to the organization, or that Relief Society is on a par with the priesthood. In 2009, the Relief Society had approximately 6 million members in over 170 countries and territories. It had no male members and not one of the 6 million women hold the priesthood. Women do not hold even the lowest order of the priesthood, that of a deacon. It is the change in the world that surrounds the church that causes the pressure to change, and their scriptures cause the difficulty to make change. The first Christian church existed three thousand years ago. What was the role of women in Old Israel? Sixty percent, seventy two million, of the women in America leave the home to go to work in 2011[50] (White House report on ABC, CBS, and NBC news, March 1, 2011). Some go to work where they are executives and may have authority over thousands of employees, and in Utah, it happens too.

In the LDS Church, it is difficult, and more so each day, to exclude woman from real authority in their religion. The female employee who exercises authority at her workplace comes home and to her church where her fifteen-year-old son, a deacon, has more true authority. Will women continue to doublethink their situation? In Relief Society, is there authority? Has a women ever been a prophet/president of the church? Has a female ever been a counselor to the president? Has a women ever been called to be one of the twelve apostles or a stake president?

Even the highest-ranking female officer, the president of the Relief Society, directs only the women of that subunit. The Relief Society is under the direction of the male authorities of the church. The president of the Relief Society has no authority over any other affairs of the church: buildings, budget (the women of the Relief Society put together a budget that is approved by a male church authority), missionary programs, investments, doctrine, etc. Without the priesthood, they do not baptize, marry couples, bless the sick, attend priesthood meetings, lead prayers in the church services, administer the sacrament, have any titles other than sister; or sit on church trials. But subservient as LDS women are today, they would not tolerate their president/prophet saying what Brigham Young once told them:

> When the servants of God in any age have consented to follow a woman for a leader, either in public or a family capacity, they have sunk beneath the standard organization had fitted them for; when a people of God submit to that, their Priesthood is taken from them, and they become as any other people.

> I shall humor the wife as far as I can consistently; and if you have any crying to do, wife, you can do that along with the children, for I have none of that kind of business to do. Let our wives be the weaker vessels, and the men be men, and show the women by their superior ability that God gives husbands wisdom and ability to lead their wives into his presence.[51] (*Journal of Discourses,* vol. 9, pp. 307–308. Quoted from *Brigham Young,* p. 347)

Take heart women of the church. It has been worse. Keep asking, "What does it mean to be human?" We will not go back three thousand years.

Mr. Lipe was the village machinist and blacksmith in Blanding. Throughout my years in San Juan County, I was constructing something. I first met him in 1961 while teaching at the Hideout. He used to add extensions to my drill bits so I could drill long holes, end to end in juniper lamps I made on a lathe, and he would sharpen my lathe tools.

Mr. Lipe was a short, stout and energetic man with a very active mind and with an opinion about nearly every issue. He was Mormon but wasn't born LDS. One day, he told me of a vision he had while he was young and building a cabin north of Blanding. He said the vision had directed him to join the church. I loved the talks with him. His jobs, which were always backed up, didn't interfere with our friendly discussions. I always drove away from his shop with admiration for his knowledge, industry, and integrity.

While principal of the San Juan Junior High School, I was building a rock home north of Blanding. One afternoon, with a project for Mr. Lipe, I was waiting at his shop for him to finish work on a middle-aged man's pickup. As the man drove off, and before I described the job I had for him, he said to me with a nod to the man driving away, "A bachelor is no good to himself or anyone else. That guy never has married." As I watched him work on the job I had given him that day, his remark about the bachelor had somewhat startled me, coming from this unassuming and generous man, but not entirely. His attitude was in line with the messages he received from church leadership. Spencer Kimball was president and the prophet of the church at the time and had this to say about bachelors.

> I shall feel sorry for this young man when he faces the Great Judge at the throne and when the Lord asks this boy: "Where is your wife?" All of his excuses, which he gave to his fellows on earth, will seem very light and senseless when he answers the Judge. "I was very busy," or "I felt I should get my education first," or "I did not find the right girl"... such answers will be hollow and of little avail.[52] (*Ensign*, February 1975, p. 2. [from *Teachings of Spencer W. Kimball*, p. 293])

The Saints are about families. Just turn on the news. In commercial time, it is the main message of the Church of Latter-day Saints. "Give your children your time." Who would argue with building strong families and devoting much time to the children? But downplayed to the world is the primary reason there is a Mormon Church, Joseph Smith being given the golden plates at the Hill Cumorah by an angel, and the angel taking the plates away from him after they were transcribed into *The Book of Mormon*. It is a tough sell to the world. It sells where it has always sold, where people are poorly educated and believe in magic and myths. Not in Cambridge, Massachusetts or Boulder, Colorado. It does best in some South American countries.

Ron Bradley lived on my floor in Helaman Halls at BYU. His mission had been to the country of South Africa in the sixties. Knowing that 80 percent of South Africa is blacks and apartheid was a rigid racial policy, I asked him if he got very many black converts. They could not hold the priesthood at that time. He said that missionaries in South Africa did not recruit the blacks, only the whites. But now, since blacks can hold the priesthood, the missionaries go for black converts. When I was at BYU, 1958 through 1962, I recall seeing only one black person on campus. He was in my comparative vertebrate anatomy class. The student population was about eleven thousand at that time. Today, there are thirty-eight thousand students, and a pitiful few are black, but understandably so.

Bachelors, old maids, gays, and lesbians have a hard time finding a niche in the Saints' church. They just don't fit with the spirit of being Mormon. Marry, have children, plenty of them—there are lots of spirit children waiting to do their time on earth—and you are on the way to the celestial kingdom. The first decade of the twenty-first century has put the Saints church once again in the nation's focus. Today, it is with their behavior toward women, and especially gays and lesbians. These groups do not have a comfortable place in Mormondom. In the years before revelations came to end polygamy and to give blacks the priesthood, church authorities excused the practices because their origin was from divine revelation. But finally, it was the outside world with its pluralism, and the demand across the land for equality that won out. Will the LDS Church find a place of equality for women, lesbians and gays? While Mormon leaders take their stand and say that the scriptures condemn homosexuality, the reality is that only the Bible says anything that could conceivably relate to homosexuality, not the Saint's scriptures.

Boyd Packer, 87, is the ranking member, president, of the Quorum of the Twelve Apostles. He is also the eldest member, and characteristic of the leadership, most are old. Attainment of leadership roles in the church with age has strengths and weaknesses. Packer represents a generation of Mormons who have not kept up with our understanding of what it means to be human. It was the LDS Church's 180th Semiannual General Conference, October 3, 2010, in Salt Lake City. More than twenty thousand people were in attendance, and millions of others watched a telecast.

Apostle Packer spoke, and his speech provoked an immediate reaction from gays and lesbians in the church and throughout that community in Utah and the nation. The LDS Church was forced to clarify its stance on these groups in the church. Packer claimed homosexuality can be corrected, and he characterized same-sex marriage as immoral. The delivery of the speech came at a time when a number of teenagers across the country had taken their own lives as a result of bullying gays. The Human Rights Campaign—in partnership with Affirmation: Gay and Lesbian Mormons, Equality Utah, and the Utah Pride Center—delivered 150,000 petitions to the church, respectfully asking Elder Boyd K. Packer, to correct his inaccurate and dangerous statements calling same-sex attraction "impure and unnatural." The petitions said,

> We're here today to tell Elder Packer, and those in the Mormon Church hierarchy who agree with him, that his statements are both factually and scientifically wrong and that more importantly, they are dangerous and are putting millions of lives in great danger. Elder Packer's assertion that sexual orientation can be changed has been debunked by both the American Psychological Association and the American Psychiatric Association. Both organizations have concluded that same-sex attraction is normal and that "reparative" therapy – like the kind being advocated by the Mormon Church—is unhealthy and harmful. Elder Packer or Church representatives have not corrected their statements in spite of the fact that they are dangerous and can result in self-loathing and potential suicide by those struggling with their sexual orientation or gender identity.[53] (www.hrcbackstory.org/2010/10/hrc-utah-leaders-deliver-150k-petitions-to-mormon-church/, "HRC & Utah Leaders Deliver 150K Petitions to Mormon Church")

The Church of Jesus Christ of Latter-day Saints issued the following statement in the *Deseret News* (LDS church owned) through a spokesman following the delivery of the petitions by the Human Rights Campaign.

> "Their struggle is our struggle," said Michael Otterson, a spokesman for The Church of Jesus Christ of Latter-

day Saints. "Those in the church who are attracted to someone of the same sex but stay faithful to the church's teachings can be happy during this life and perform meaningful service in the church.

"They can enjoy full fellowship with other church members including attending and serving in temples, and ultimately receive all the blessings afforded to those who live the commandments of God."

The LDS Church recognizes that those of its members who are attracted to the same sex experience have deep emotional, social and physical feelings," Otterson said.

"The church distinguishes between feelings or inclinations on one hand, and behavior on the other," he said. "It's not a sin to have feelings, only in yielding to temptation"[54] (*Deseret News*, Oct. 12, 2010, by Scott Taylor, "Mormon church reiterates its stance on marriage in response to petition from gay rights group").

The Saints' leadership takes its position. They acknowledge the attraction by gays for gays and lesbians for lesbians, but their position is, "Don't practice homosexuality." To practice it is a sin. If you actively practice homosexuality, you won't get to the celestial heaven. You won't get the bishop's recommendation to do the temple rituals. At BYU, being an active homosexual student, faculty member, or staff member will cause dismissal. However, the code states,

One's stated same-gender attraction is not an Honor Code issue. However, the Honor Code requires all members of the university community to manifest a strict commitment to the law of chastity. Homosexual behavior is inappropriate and violates the Honor Code.

> Homosexual behavior includes not only sexual relations
> between members of the same sex, but all forms of
> physical intimacy that give expression to homosexual
> feelings.[55] (www.saas.byu.edu/catalog/20102011ucat/
> GeneralInfo/HonorCode.php, BYU Honor Code,
> Homosexual Behavior)

The BYU chastity code made national attention two seasons ago when the star center, Brandon Daives, a black man, told the coach he had sex with his girlfriend. He was dismissed from the team for the rest of the season. BYU had been ranked third in the nation. Dave Rose, the coach, said, "Brandon's heart is in the right place, I think that he wants to continue his education here at BYU." A year before Daives's dismissal, the star running back for BYU's football team, Harvey Unga, had to withdraw from the school along with his girlfriend, a basketball player for the college's women's team, because they were having sex. The couple had been dating for three years, and they later married.

There are nearly 7 billion humans on the planet. The Church of Jesus Christ of Latter-day Saints reported nearly 14 million worldwide members on record in October 2010. Most of us who are living are left out of the LDS church privileges which include reaching the highest glory in heaven, but not all the dead are left out. The Saints baptize them so they may get to heaven. It is part of the church mission. Following is the explanation given by the LDS Church.

> Because all who have lived on the earth have not had the
> opportunity to be baptized by proper authority during
> life on earth, baptisms may be performed by proxy,
> meaning a living person may be baptized in behalf of a

deceased person. Baptisms for the dead are performed by Church members in temples throughout the world. People have occasionally wondered if the mortal remains of the deceased are somehow disturbed in this process; they are not. The person acting as a proxy uses only the name of the deceased. To prevent duplication, the Church keeps a record of the deceased persons who have been baptized. Some have misunderstood that when baptisms for the dead are performed, the names of deceased persons are being added to the membership records of the Church. This is not the case.[56] (mormon. org/faq/baptism-for-the-dead/, "Why do Mormons perform baptisms for the dead?")

Baptism of the dead happens without acknowledgement of the findings by archaeologist and anthropologists that Cro-Magnon people of Europe, who were doing well forty thousand years ago, were humans. If attired in today's clothing, these people would not be identified as Cro-Magnon in a mall. Our species that were living in many regions of the world forty thousand years ago would probably get along in our schools. Human evolution is slow relative to historical time. Forty thousand years in earth time may not produce significant physiological changes at all. But all the humans that have lived from forty thousand years ago would be billions, and there would be no records of the individuals except those of the last few centuries, at most.

Are Mormons who baptize the dead ancestors unaware of the real challenge, or are they just following Joseph Smith's directions? They spend cumulatively centuries of time tracing their ancestors and baptizing them so they can enter into heaven. LDS genealogical records are unequaled. But how far do historical records allow them to go back, three hundred, four hundred years, or perhaps, with noble ancestry, five hundred years? What a tiny portion of human ancestry they will baptize, even if they found every record of a life. It started with Joseph Smith. Of course, their ideal is to get back to Abraham, Noah, and, finally, to Adam and Eve.

But that is Old Testament stuff, and it excludes all the other hundreds of centuries of humans, unless of course, you exclude geology, archeology, and anthropology, and believe the earth is six thousand years old. And the Saints do not know if the dead want to be baptized. They got into spiritual trouble that turned to legal trouble when they were baptizing long-dead Jews[57] (www.jewishgen.org/infofiles/ldsagree.html, "The Issue of the Mormon Baptisms of Jewish Holocaust Victims and Other Jewish Dead").

It was the summer of 1989. I attended a workshop at Georgetown University in Washington DC. I was paid to attend by a maker of biological equipment. The purpose of the workshop was to learn DNA technology so the technology could be used in advanced biology classes in high schools. The company wanted to broaden their market. In attendance were a few professors of science education like myself and many more high school biology teachers from across the nation. Georgetown University is a short distance south on Wisconsin Avenue from the National Institute of Health where work was beginning on a project that equaled our man-on-the-moon landing.

The NIH and many universities were working together to figure out the human genome, the genes that make up the directions for making and operating a human. In the morning classes, we studied molecular biology, and in the afternoon, we did labs that used the chemicals and equipment that allowed us to, among other things, DNA projects, identify human DNA strands and family lines. DNA identification is many times more specific than a fingerprint. It has revolutionized the anthropological study of the geographic origin of peoples. The technology can separate Flannigans of Ireland from the Irish Kellys. Early on, I saw another application.

It would interest the Mormons, or may be frightening to the Saints, to settle once and for all where the American Indians, their Lamanites, came from, Siberia or the Middle East. Only a few years later, a Mormon molecular biologist in Australia, Simon E. Southerton, who had been an LDS bishop, undertook the project. In 1998, before the DNA study began, his religion and his science conflicted, and he renounced the LDS religion. In 2004, the accomplished biologist published the book, *Losing a Lost Tribe,* with elaboration about his changed view of Mormonism. It is the scientific death knell to the Joseph Smith story about the Israeli origin of America's Indians. Southerton's DNA study takes the origin of Americans Indians, as suspected from much earlier archeological evidence and bloodline studies, to southern Siberia. Southerton says in a lengthy message to the public, but especially to Mormons, concerning the lack of DNA evidence for Israelites as the progenitors of American Indians,

> The truth is that there is no reliable scientific evidence supporting migrations from the Middle East to the New World, just as the Smithsonian statement had said. Some Mormon scholars and indeed Apostles are aware of this and quietly acknowledge it in academic circles behind closed doors. This is never revealed to the Church at large presumably because it isn't faith promoting.[58] (www.exmormon.org/whylft125.htm)

The Southerton study seems to have had little or no repercussions with the faithful. It should change the story. Lamanites should now be with the "ins." But the thousands of missionaries are out there, knocking on doors, telling the world how the Americas were peopled, and in testimony meetings around the world, the Saints tell each other Smith's message is true. They know it in their heart. A footnote: at Point of the Mountain, the Utah state prison, DNA evidence can be used to take lives of criminals.

Whoa there! Southerton's study is not the absolute answer to the peopling of the American continents. With the word absolute, science and most religions divide. Science functions with degrees of certainty, not absolutes. Jacob Bronownski, author of *The Ascent of Man*, said it best. "There is no absolute knowledge, and those who proclaim it, open the door to tragedy. All information is imperfect." Mormonism has absolutes, but so do most religions. And most religions have members who would die for their absolute truths. Many Mormon "heart truths" are absolutes, and they famously confound the believers. I'll go with reason. As Ben Franklin said, "The way to see by faith is to shut the eye of reason." In our new world where our lives depend upon the achievements of science, the faithful of nearly all religions acknowledge their faith in the reasoning of science. Where do the victims of cancer, heart problems, and all other medical problems go with knowledge of their problem? To medical scientists who reason about solutions.

I love the Four Corners Country. As I have described, it is the geological Mecca, the greatest expose of earth's geological history and the history of some of the continent's first inhabitants. To this I will add, it has wonderful climate with four distinct seasons. In Blanding one could be honest, honorable, and support values that are American, but it wasn't enough. We were still out because we were not in the church. Do you belong? It remains the question of religious and social approval in Blanding and much of Utah. I couldn't bear to see my young children grow up under such social conditions.

My daughter, Julie, received her PhD in cultural anthropology from the University of Minnesota a few summers ago and is now a professor at the University of Wisconsin–Eau Claire. I have made a few good decisions, and a few bad ones along the way, like we all have. But the best decision I ever made was to leave southern Utah, especially Blanding. It was my thirteenth year in Zion. Let me add more that was ominous, specific, and personal to the decision to leave.

It was in the early spring of 1975, our family's last year in Utah, and activities were turning to the outdoors again. Julie was in the second grade. She and another second grader, a little Mormon girl, were very good friends. Julie talked about Jill often and said she and Jill finished things first at school. They were the class scholars, and Julie's scholarship continues today. There was friendly competition, and after school, they walked together to their homes. Jill's home was two blocks farther south. The routine in reverse happened each morning. At home with Julie, it was "Jill and I this," and "Jill and I that."

Shortly after beginning the Blanding job, we decided to build a rock home up north of Blanding by Devil's Canyon. In Mormondom to build a home near "Devil's Canyon" probably inadvertently was to put one strike against us gentiles. It is so beautiful there on the north rim of the canyon, about eight miles north of Blanding. It's on the southeast

side of the Abaho Mountains, and from the home, one can see three of
the Four Corners states, including the Ship Rock in New Mexico.

One gorgeous spring evening, my family decided to drive to the home
site for a few hours of construction. But we needed gasoline in the
pickup. We headed south down the road in front of our rented home
to get the gas. On the low chain link fence at Jill's home, completely
circling the front yard, were balloons and a sign saying, "Happy Birthday
Jill." There were probably thirty children playing in the front yard. Julie
was so quiet as we passed by the home. By the time we reached the gas
station, she was crying. Neither my wife nor I knew how to explain it to
her. We continued to our new house location and worked that evening
with hardly a word to say. After a late dinner and Julie and Tim were
in bed, I told my wife, "We have to get out of here."

Jill's Primary teacher, the Mormon equivalent of Sunday School, planned
that party with Jill's mother. They were oblivious to the non-Mormon
families in the town. Probably, there were not more than six or eight.
Their church was the institution of most value to them, and everyone
who didn't belong to it should belong to it, in their minds. Once again,
the first identity of so many Mormons is that they are Mormon, not that
they are first, members of the human family. It was not little Jill's fault.
She probably was not even consulted. She had already accepted it as the
Mormon way. The next day, my search for another position began.

We left the glorious Four Corners Country. I knew of another world
beyond Zion. But what of the Mormon school principal whose life
and his family's life and all of their friends were in the church. What
if he discovered one morning that he was no longer a believer and had
become an apostate? We exercised freedom with few regrets, apologies,

or social losses. Could the principal or a woman with five children locked into the church/culture support system do the same?

I only return to Blanding as a tourist, and not for long. But along with the bitter taste, there was good for me in thirteen years with the Saints. Most important is the way I cherish freedom. There are many ways to lose one's freedom. Religions and governments can take it away. Before giving up any freedoms, analyze the cause and the price.

Tangential and unrelated to Blanding society or the LDS Church, I must tell of my son, Tim. He is multiply handicapped with a degenerative central nervous system disease and lives in a group home in Laramie with special help. Near to Denver, he has the best care. This is not to imply that the LDS neglect their handicapped.

And for Julie, in Laramie, Wyoming, she completed the rest of the grades through a master's degree in international studies at the University of Wyoming. I like to think that her three years in Blanding in our minority situation triggered her desire to be sensitive to all cultures. At our first parent conference after she entered the third grade in Laramie, her teacher was set back by the fact she was reading Alex Halely's *Roots*. The TV adaptation was on at the time. Before she was twenty-four, she had been to China three times and completed her master's degree with a study of Mongolian rural medicine. Her PhD study was about the difficult cultural adaptation of Hmong people into the United States following the Vietnam War. Her doctoral thesis was published in book form. She speaks four languages. In Laramie, there were always students of many nationalities in her classes and in her home. Her wedding was high in the Snowy Range Mountains at a chapel where one can see east across the Laramie plains, almost to Nebraska. There were Navajo

Indians there, and two Arapaho Indians, Chinese, Mexican Americans, and African Americans, who had become the bride and groom's friends along the way.

What were possible outcomes of Julie's life growing up in the closed society of Blanding and possibly marrying there? You know love; it makes some bedeviling entanglements. Which church should our children attend? Could they not attend any church? Could they be agnostic? Don't you know there is only one true church? Aren't you going to be married in the LDS temple? Julie, your children should go to Primary. You should have a large family. Oh my, the conflicts. And the guilt trips laid on kids and their parents by the Saints. In the second grade, a note was passed to Julie that said she would go to hell because she didn't attend Primary.

With observance of Mormon scriptures, we would all be living in very separate caves today, believing God had us separated. But it is just the opposite.

Science has abolished distance, and we all live in one cave now, our little shrunken globe on which there is a place for only one family, the family of man.
—Albert Szent Gyorgi

POSTSCRIPT

Perhaps the whole book is a postscript, a look back at the thirteen years in Zion. Time, age, and education have mellowed my anger, especially toward the little town of Blanding, which for years would cause me to lose sleep. Thirty years to reflect before writing these thoughts have allowed me to "give 'em a break." Mormonism was in its beginning and is today a unique social and religious adventure. Many of the scriptures that bound the pioneers of the faith have unparalleled absurdity, but around their scriptures, Saints built a society that was enduring through great adversity.

Today, it seems brittle and ready to break against the onslaught of science, multiculturalism, and demands for human rights. Throughout the book, I hope I have not failed to point out that Mormonism is a vivid case, an extreme exemplar case, of irrationality that is in all religions. Mormonism is so vulnerable because its scriptures are so new and the erosion by time does not allow the believers, or the critics from the outside, to deny what Joseph Smith with his scribes put to paper. It is hard to view Mormon scriptures as symbolic or allegorical.

Religions have zealots who look to their scriptures for answers to questions science and the information age have explained with reason. But science has zealots too. Science zealots want to leave religion without a role in a meaningful life. As my philosopher friend and scientist Jeff Lockwood said to me, "Is irrationality such an awful price to pay for the benefits of assuredness, community and meaning? These seem to be increasingly rare in modern society." Life is more secure if the answers are known. Can science be a measure of all realms of humanity?

Maybe some of us are born free, but more likely, one must know freedom and lose it to know it. Missionaries I have known who return to Utah give a sigh of relief. But it isn't for freedom regained having left the gentile world. It is their familiarity and security with the LDS cultural system. When the walls of communism came down, many Russians missed the security the old USSR gave them, having never known freedom. The Mormon missionary life by its rules is so monastic that the familiarity of Utah is freedom.

For my family, following the years in Blanding, the move to Wyoming seemed like the escape to Wyoming. True democracy is notoriously disobedient, and we had missed disobedience in Utah. My daughter and I missed disobedience and freedom while in the USSR in 1985. We had been a week in communistic Russia with an education group and flew from Leningrad (now Saint Petersburg) to Helsinki, Finland. The guide who met our group said to us, as we descended from the plane onto the tarmac, "Welcome to the free world." We knew it. We could feel it.

At a Wyoming football game, in the fall of the first year in Wyoming, I looked around and noticed the disobedience, not so much in the language or disrespect for the opposing team—although a BYU basketball coach called UW fans despicable—it was dress, a swear word, smell of beer, the lack of tension for not being like the Mormon Church would have us be. There were times at that first football game when I wanted to stand up like dear Martin and say, "I'm free, I'm free, I'm free at last."

WORKS CITED

1. *Documentary History of the Church,* vol. IV, p. 461.

2. "The Age of the Earth and Universe," George O. Abell, *Scientists Confront Creationists,* pp. 34–35, W. W. Norton & Company, 1983.

3. *The Book of Mormon,* Moroni, 10:4.

4. *History of the Church,* vol. III, p. 29, publication of the LDS Church.

5. *No Man Knows My History,* Fawn Brodie, p. 39, Alfred A. Knopf, 1945, and lds.org/scriptures/pgp/js-h/1.30-32?lang=eng#29 (LDS website).

6. *National Geographic Magazine,* p. 219, August 1972.

7. *The Heavens Resound: A History of the Latter-day Saints in Ohio, 1830– 1838,* Milton V. Backman Jr., p. 140, Deseret Books, 1983.

8. "*The Book of Mormon* – Keystone of Our Religion," Ezra Taft Benson, *Ensign,* November 1986, p. 4.

9. *Darwin's Century,* Loren Eisley, p. 292, Doubleday, 1958.

10. "New Light: Smithsonian Statement on the Book of Mormon

Revisited," in the Mormon journal, *Journal of Book of Mormon Studies*, vol. 7, issue 1, p. 77, 1998.

11. "What Utah Children Believe," Duane Keown, *The Humanist*, July/August issue 1986, pp. 21–26.

12. "The Impossible Voyage of Noah's Ark," Robert Moore, *Creation/ Evolution*, winter issue, 1983.

13. *Doctrine and Covenants*, 84:14–17.

14. Popperian Idea, *The Logic of Scientific Discovery*, Karl Popper, 1959.

15. www.wikipedia.org/wiki/Largest_organisms.

16. *Noah and the Flood*, Mark E. Petersen, p. 65, Deseret Books, 1982.

17. "This is Not the Place," Hampton Sides, *Double Take Magazine*, Spring 1999.

18. www.irr.org/mit/bom-arch-v1.html#Endnote%2021, Michael Coe on *The Book of Mormon.*

19. www.en.wikipedia.org/wiki/Book_of_Abraham, Figures on the Egyptian scrolls.

20. *Pearl of Great Price.* Abraham 1:21–26, Mormon Holy Scripture Book.

21. *The Denver Post, (Empire Magazine)*, p. 17, p. 20–28, 1982.

22. www.lds-mormon.com/legrand_richards.shtml, website of the LDS Church, interview with Apostle LeGrand Richards, by Wesley P. Walters and Chris Vlachos, August 16, 1978, Church Office Building (recorded on cassette).

23. *The Denver Post, (Empire Magazine)*, p. 20, Nov. 28, 1982.

24. *Journal of Discourses*, pp. 55–57, vol. 4.

25. www/ lds.org/scriptures/dc-testament/od/1?lang=eng (President

Woodruff prepares the Saints to abandon polygamy, website of the LDS Church, as reported in *Deseret Weekly*, November 14, 1891.

26. *Los Angeles Times*, October 1, 1981.

27. www.earthtrends.wri.org/text/energy-resources/variable-351.html.

28. "The Church's Growth, Structure and Reach," *The Mormons*.PBS.org. April 2007.

29. www.worldometers.info, World Population Numbers.

30. www.prb.org/.../HumanPopulation/PopulationGrowth.aspx—Cached—Similar; Population Reference Bureau—Google

31. *Modern Biology*, by James H. Otto and Albert Towle, Holt, Rinehart and Winston, 1973.

32. "Growthville, Wyoming," *Wild Wonderful Wyoming* (Secondary Activities Manual), Duane Keown, University of Wyoming, 1998.

33. R. A. Hamond, *Deseret News*, April 29, 1885, the Salt Lake Mormon newspaper.

34. Keynote address at the Red Desert Rendezvous, Rock Springs, Wy, June 18, 2011.

35. www.preservationnation.org/issues/public-lands/bureau-of-land-management/san-juan-county.html, Anasazi Ruins of San Juan County, Utah.

36. "Earth as a One Year Movie," *Wild Wonderful Wyoming* (Secondary Activities Manual), Duane Keown and David Rizor, University of Wyoming, 1998.

37. "Human Evolution by the Smithsonian Institution's Human Origins Program," *Human Origins Initiative*, Smithsonian Institution. Retrieved 08/30/2010.

38. "Global Health Threats: Global Warming in Perspective,"

IndruGoklalny, *Journal of American Physicians and Surgeons*, Fall 2009.

39. www.utahcleanenergy.org/clean_energy_101/wind_101#wind_ potential, Utah Clean Energy.

40. Commencement Address at the University of Portland, Paul Hawken, May 2009.

41. *The Psychological and Ethical Aspects of Mormon Group Life*, Ephraim Edward Erickson, p. 28, The University of Utah Press, 1975.

42. *Doctrine and Covenants*, Section 1:35–36.

43. wikipedia.org/wiki/Mountain_Meadows_massacre, *The Mountain Meadows Massacre* by Juanita Brooks, Stanford University Press, 1950; and *Blood of the Prophets* by Will Bagley, University of Oklahoma Press, 2002.

44. *The Rocky Mountain Saints*, T.H.B. Stenhouse, p. XXII, Appleton & Company, 1873.

45. *The Mormon Experience*, Leonard J. Arrington and Davis Bitton, p. 122, Alfred A. Knopf, 1979.

46. *Doctrine and Covenants*, Section 127:3

47. *New America*, William H. Dixon, pp. 171–173, J.B. Lippincott & Co., 1869.

48. *From Housewife to Heretic*, Sonia Johnson, pp. 383–384, Doubleday & Company, 1981.

49. www. mormon.org/faq/women-in-the-church/-cached (website of the LDS Church), Gordon Hinckley, "Why don't women hold the priesthood in the Mormon Church? How do women lead in the Mormon Church?"

50. White House report on ABC, CBS, and NBC news, March 1, 2011.

51. *Journal of Discourses,* vol. 9, pp. 307–308. Quoted from *BrighamYoung,* p. 347.

52. *Ensign,* February 1975, p. 2 (from *Teachings of Spencer W. Kimball,* p. 293).

53. www.hrcbackstory.org/2010/10/hrc-utah-leaders-deliver-150k-petitions-to-mormon-church/, "HRC & Utah Leaders Deliver 150K Petitions to Mormon Church."

54. *Deseret News,* Oct. 12, 2010, by Scott Taylor, "Mormon church reiterates its stance on marriage in response to petition from gay rights group."

55. www.saas.byu.edu/catalog/2010-2011ucat/GeneralInfo/HonorCode.php, BYU Honor Code, Homosexual Behavior

56. wwwmormon.org/faq/baptism-for-the-dead/ (website of the LDS Church), "Why do Mormons perform baptisms for the dead?"

57. www.jewishgen.org/infofiles/ldsagree.html, "The Issue of the Mormon Baptisms of Jewish Holocaust Victims and Other Jewish Dead."

58. www.exmormon.org/whylft125.htm, Simon Southerton, "DNA Genealogies of American Indians and the *Book of Mormon,*" March 17, 2000.

CPSIA information can be obtained at www.ICGtesting.com
Printed in the USA
LVOW040455201112

307985LV00001B/6/P